BY YIYUN LI

Dear Friend, from My Life I Write to You in Your Life

Kinder Than Solitude

Gold Boy, Emerald Girl

The Vagrants

A Thousand Years of Good Prayers

Dear Friend,
from My Life
I Write to You
in Your Life

RANDOM HOUSE
NEW YORK

Dear Friend, from My Life I Write to You in Your Life

Yiyun Li

Published in the United States by Random House, an imprint and division of Penguin Random House LLC, New York.

RANDOM HOUSE and the HOUSE colophon are registered trademarks of Penguin Random House LLC.

"Dear Friend, from My Life I Write to You in Your Life" was originally published in A Public Space and reprinted in The Best American Essays 2014.

Grateful acknowledgment is made to the following for permission to reprint previously published material:

Alfred Music: Excerpt from "Five Hundred Miles," words and music by Hedy West, copyright © 1964 (Renewed) Unichappell Music, Inc., and Atzal Music, Inc. All rights administered by Unichappell Music, Inc. All rights reserved. Used by permission of Alfred Music.

Faber and Faber Limited: Excerpt from Letters to Monica by Philip Larkin, edited by Anthony Thwaite. Philip Larkin's letters copyright © 2010 by the Estate of Philip Larkin; Monica Jones's letters copyright © 2010 by the Estate of Monica Jones; selection, introduction, and editorial matter copyright © 2010 by Anthony Thwaite. Reprinted by permission of Faber and Faber Limited.

Alfred A. Knopf, an imprint of the Knopf Doubleday Publishing Group, a division of Penguin Random House LLC, and A. M. Heath & Co. Ltd.: Excerpts from All Will Be Well: A Memoir by John McGahern, copyright © 2005 by John McGahern. Rights in Canada are controlled by A. M. Heath & Co. Ltd. Reprinted by permission of Alfred A. Knopf, an imprint of the Knopf Doubleday Publishing Group, a division of Penguin Random House LLC, and A. M. Heath & Co. Ltd.

LIBRARY OF CONGRESS CATALOGING-IN-PUBLICATION DATA
Names: Li, Yiyun, author.
Title: Dear friend, from my life I write to you in your life / Yiyun Li.
Description: First edition. | New York : Random House, 2017.
Identifiers: LCCN 2016017675| ISBN 9780399589096 (hardback) | ISBN 9780399589119 (ebook)
Subjects: LCSH: Li, Yiyun, 1972– —Mental health. | Authors, American—21st century—Biography. | Depressed persons—United States—Biography. | Autobiography. | BISAC: BIOGRAPHY & AUTOBIOGRAPHY / Personal Memoirs. | LITERARY COLLECTIONS / Essays. | PSYCHOLOGY / Psychopathology / Depression.
Classification: LCC PS3612.I16 Z46 2017 | DDC 813/.6 [B]—dc23
LC record available at https://lccn.loc.gov/2016017675

Printed in the United States of America on acid-free paper

randomhousebooks.com

9 8 7 6 5 4 3 2 1

First Edition

This book is part of a conversation with Brigid Hughes.

There is no ladder out of any world; each world is rimless.

—Amy Leach, *Things That Are*

She had always enjoyed waking people who were asleep; and indeed it is as great an alteration to the state of a fellow-creature that we can make short of killing them or giving birth to them.

—Rebecca West, *This Real Night*

Contents

Dear Friend,
from My Life
I Write to You
in Your Life

Dear Friend, from My Life I Write to You in Your Life

1.

My first encounter with *before and after* was in one of the fashion magazines my friends told me to subscribe to when I came to America. I duly followed their advice—I had an anthropologist's fascination with America then. I had never seen a glossy magazine, and the print and paper quality, not to mention the trove of perfumes waiting to be unfolded, made me wonder how the economics of the magazine worked, considering I paid no more than a dollar for an issue.

My favorite column was on the last page of the magazine, and it featured celebrity makeovers—hairstyle and hair color, for instance—with two bubbles signifying before and after. I didn't often have an opinion about the transformation, but I liked the definitiveness of that phrase, *before and after,* with nothing muddling the in-between.

After years of living in America, I still feel a momentary elation whenever I see advertisements for weight-loss programs, teeth-whitening strips, hair-loss treatments, or plastic surgery with the contrasting effects shown under *before* and *after.* The certainty in that pronouncement— for each unfortunate or inconvenient situation, there is a solution to make it no longer be—both attracts and perplexes me. Life can be reset, it seems to say; time can be separated. But that logic appears to me as unlikely as traveling to another place to become a different person. Altered sceneries are at best distractions, or else new settings for old habits. What one carries from one point to another, geographically or temporally, is one's self. Even the most inconsistent person is consistently himself.

2.

I was leaving to teach class when an acquaintance who lived across the country in New Hampshire called my office. She had traveled to a nearby city. I talked to her for no more than two minutes before telling my husband to go find her. He spent twelve hours with her, canceled her business appointments, and saw to it that she flew back home. Two weeks later her husband called and said she had jumped out of her office on a Sunday evening. He asked me to attend her memorial service. I thought for a long time and decided not to.

Our memories tell more about now than then. Doubt-less the past is real. There is no shortage of evidence: pho-tos, journals, letters, old suitcases. But we choose and discard from an abundance of evidence what suits us at the moment. There are many ways to carry the past with us: to romanticize it, to invalidate it, to furnish it with revised or entirely fictionalized memories. The present does not surrender so easily to manipulation.

I don't want the present to judge the past, so I don't want to ponder my absence at her memorial service. We had come to this country around the same time. When I told her that I was going to quit science to become a writer, she seemed curious, but her husband said that it was a grave mistake. Why do you want to make your life difficult? he asked.

3.

I have had a troublesome relationship with time. The past I cannot trust because it could be tainted by my memory. The future is hypothetical and should be treated with caution. The present—what is the present but a constant test: in this muddled in-between one struggles to under-stand what about oneself has to be changed, what ac-cepted, what preserved. Unless the right actions are taken, one seems never to pass the test to reach the after.

4.

After the second of two hospital stays following a difficult time, I went to a program for those whose lives have fallen apart. Often someone would say—weeping, shaking, or dry eyed—that he or she wished to go back in time and make everything right again.

I wished, too, that life could be reset, but reset from when? From each point I could go to an earlier point: warning signs neglected, mistakes aggregated, but it was useless to do so, as I often ended up with the violent wish that I had never been born.

I was quiet most of the time, until I was told I was evasive and not making progress. But my pain was my private matter, I thought; if I could understand and articulate my problems I wouldn't have been there in the first place.

Do you want to share anything, I was prompted when I had little to offer. By then I felt my hope had run out. I saw the revolving door admitting new people and letting old people out into the world; similar stories were told with the same remorse and despair; the lectures were on the third repeat. What if I were stuck forever in that basement room? I broke down and could feel a collective sigh: my tears seemed to prove that finally I intended to cooperate.

I had only wanted to stay invisible, but there as elsewhere invisibility is a luxury.

5.

I have been asked throughout my life: What are you hiding? I don't know what I am hiding, and the more I try to deny it, the less trustworthy people find me. My mother used to comment on my stealthiness to our guests. A woman in charge of admission at the public bathhouse often confronted me, asking what I was hiding from her. Nothing, I said, and she would say she could tell from my eyes that I was lying.

Reticence is a natural state. It is not hiding. People don't show themselves equally and easily to all. Reticence doesn't make one feel lonely as hiding does, yet it distances and invalidates others.

6.

There are five time zones in China, but the nation uses a unified time—Beijing time. When the hour turns, all radio stations sound six beeps, followed by a solemn announcement: "At the last beep, it is Beijing time seven o'clock sharp." This memory is reliable because it does not belong to me but to generations of Chinese people, millions of us: every hour, the beeping and the announcement were amplified through loudspeakers in every People's Commune, school, army camp, and apartment complex.

But underneath this steadfastness, time is both intrusive and elusive. It does not leave us alone even in our most private moments. In every thought and feeling about life, time claims a space. When we speak of indecision, we are unwilling to let go of a present. When we speak of moving on—what a triumphant phrase—we are cutting off the past. And if one seeks kindness from time, it slips away tauntingly, or worse, with indifference. How many among us have said that to others or to ourselves: if only I had a bit more time . . .

7.

One hides something for two reasons: either one feels protective of it or one feels ashamed of it. And it is not always the case that the two possibilities can be separated. If my relationship with time is difficult, if time is intrusive and elusive, could it be that I am only hiding myself from time?

I used to write from midnight to four o'clock. I had young children then, various jobs (from working with mice to working with cadaver tissue to teaching writing), and an ambition to keep writing separate from my *real* life. When most people were being ferried across the night by sleep, unaware of time, unaware of weather, I felt the luxury of living on the cusp of reality.

Night for those sound sleepers was a cocoon against time. For me, I wanted to believe, it was even better. Time, at night, was my possession, not the other way around.

8.

A friend came to see me when I visited Beijing in 2008. We talked about her real estate investments and our old schoolmates. Half an hour after she left my parents' apartment, she called. She hadn't wanted to mention it in person, but a boy who had been close to me when we were teenagers had committed suicide, along with a lover.

My first reaction was wonderment, that my friend would wait until we were out of each other's sight to tell me. My next reaction was still wonderment, as though I had always been waiting for this news.

Our dead friend had had an affair, and both he and the woman had gone through difficult divorces only to be ostracized as adulterers.

It'd have been better had he gone to America, my friend said.

Why, I asked. In college he had already been doing well as a self-taught designer. Often he would include with his letters cutout ads from newspapers and magazines: brand-name garments, imported mints, cashmeres. He was someone who would have made a good life in the country's developing economy.

My friend sighed. You're the only one more impractical than he was, she said; you should know this is not a country for dreamers.

My friendship with the boy existed largely in correspondence. It was a different era, thoughts and feelings traveling by mail, urgency conveyed by telegrams. My family did not have a telephone until I was in college; email came much later, when I was in America. I still remember the days when the engine of a motorcycle disturbed the quietest night—only a telegram announcing a death or a looming one would permit such an intrusion. Letters, especially those bearing too many stamps, carried the weight of friendship.

I can recall only a few things from those letters: a crush on the girl sitting next to him in class; a Chekhovian political satire he wrote, featuring Gorbachev and an East German general and a pistol going off in act 3—this was in 1988, and Communism still retained its hold on part of Europe. It was in that year too that we last saw each other.

But I do remember that before he found an outlet for his artistic obsession and sent those profitable ads, he had dreamed up, designed, and named endless car models; there had also been odd assortments of pistols, rifles, spacecraft, and household appliances, as well as abstract graphics. All the drawings were meticulously done, sometimes in their fifth or sixth drafts, and their detail used to fill me with awe and impatience.

Perhaps when I say I was expecting his suicide, it is only memory going back to revise itself. There is no reason an artistic and sensitive boy could not grow into a happy man. Where and how things went amiss with him I do not know, though even as a teenager, I recognized his despondency when at school the production of his play earned him jeers and a special exhibition of his car designs estranged him from his classmates. He was the kind of person who needed others to feel his existence.

9.

A dreamer: it's the last thing I want to be called, in China or in America. No doubt when my friend in Beijing used the term, she was thinking of traits like persistence, single-mindedness, willfulness, and—particularly—impracticality, which she must have seen plenty of in me. Still, that one possesses a dreamer's personality and that one has dreams do not guarantee that one knows how to dream.

The woman in New Hampshire and I, and many like us, came to this country with the same goal—to make a new life here. I wouldn't call it a dream, not even an ambition. She had followed the scientist's path and had a secure job at a biomedical company. I had drifted away, choosing a profession that makes hiding less feasible, if indeed I am a habitual hider.

I don't wonder what my life would have been had I stayed in China: not leaving had never felt like an option. For a decade there had been a concrete after ingrained in everything I did. The day I arrived in America I would become a new person.

But there is the possibility that I might never have taken up writing. Had I remained a scientist, would I have turned out differently—calmer, less troubled, more sensible? Would I have stopped hiding, or become better at it?

10.

A few months before my friend's suicide, he had found me on the Internet. In his email he told me about his divorce, and I told him about giving up science for writing. He wrote back, "I congratulate you. You've always been a dreamer, but America has made your dream come true."

Someone described me onstage as an example of the American dream. Certainly I have done that too, putting myself on a poster of before and after. The transformation, however, is as superficial and deceitful as an ad placed on the back of a bus.

Time will tell, people say, as though time always has the last word. Perhaps I am only hiding from time as I have been hiding from those who want the power to have the last word about others.

11.

I would have liked to be called a dreamer had I known how to dream. The sense of being an imposter, I understand, occurs naturally, and those who do not occasionally feel so I find untrustworthy. I would not mind being taken as many things I am not: a shy person, a cheerful person, a cold person. But I do not want to be called a dreamer when I am far from being a real one.

12.

What I admire and respect in a dreamer: her confidence in her capacities, her insusceptibility to the frivolous, and her faith that the good and the real shall triumph and last. There is nothing selfish, dazzling, or preposterous about dreamers; in everyday life they blend in rather than stand out, though it's not hiding. A real dreamer has a mutual trust with time.

Apart from feeling unqualified to be called a dreamer, I may also be worrying about being mistaken for one of those who call themselves dreamers but are merely ambitious. One meets them often in life, their ambitions smaller than dreams, more commonplace, in need of broadcasting and dependent on recognition from this particular time. If they cause pain to others, they have no trouble writing off those damages as the cost of their dreams. Timeliness may be one thing that separates ambitions from real dreams.

13.

The woman in New Hampshire was neither a dreamer nor an ambitious person. She had hoped for a solid and uneventful life in an American suburb, but loneliness must have made her life a desert.

My dead friend in Beijing was ambitious because he understood his talents; he had dreams, too. I must have been part of his dreams once—why else would he have written if not to seek kinship with another dreamer.

14.

I came to this country as an aspiring immunologist. I had chosen the field—if one does not count the practical motives of wanting a reason to leave China and of having a skill to make a living—because I had liked the working concept of the immune system. Its job is to detect and attack nonself; it has memories, some as long lasting as life; its memories can go awry selectively, or, worse, indiscriminately, leading the system to mistake self as foreign, as something to eliminate. The word *immune* (from the Latin *immunis, in-* + *munia*, services, obligations) is among my favorites in the English language, the possession of immunity—to illnesses, to follies, to love and loneliness and troubling thoughts and unalleviated pains—a trait that I have desired for my characters and myself, knowing all the while the futility of such a wish. Only the lifeless can be immune to life.

15.

One's intuition is to acquire immunity to those who confirm one's beliefs about life, and to those who turn one's beliefs into nothing. The latter are the natural predators of our hearts, the former made into enemies because we are, unlike other species, capable of not only enlarging but also diminishing our precarious selves.

16.

I had this notion, when I first started writing this, that it would be a way to test—to assay—thoughts about time. There was even a vision of an after, when my confusions would be sorted out.

Assays in science are part of an endless exploration. One question leads to another; what follows confirms or disconfirms what comes before. To assay one's ideas about time while time remains unsettled and elusive feels futile. Just as one is about to understand one facet of time, it presents another to undermine one's reasoning.

To write about a struggle amid the struggling: one must hope that this muddling will end someday.

17.

But what more do you want? You have a family, a profession, a house, a car, friends, and a place in the world. Why can't you be happy? Why can't you be strong? These questions are asked, among others, by my mother.

There was a majestic mental health worker in the second hospital where I stayed who came to work with perfect lipstick, shining curly hair, and bright blouses and flats of matching colors.

Young lady, she said every time she saw me; don't lose that smile of yours.

I had liked her, and liked her still after she questioned my spiritual life. I could see that the godless state of my mind concerned her, and that my compliance made me a good project. Don't mind her, my roommate, a black Buddhist, said; she has an evangelical background. I don't, I assured my roommate; being preached to did not bother me.

Then I had a difficult day. At dinnertime, the majestic woman asked, Young lady, why did you cry today?

I'm sad, I said.

We know you're sad. What I want to know is, what makes you sad?

Can't I just be left alone in my sadness? I said. The women around the table smiled into their plates. The good girl was having a tantrum.

18.

What makes you sad? What makes you angry? What makes you forget the good things in your life and your responsibilities toward others? One hides from people who ask these unanswerable questions only to ask them oneself again and again.

I know you don't like me to ask what's brought you here, my roommate said, but can you describe how you feel? I don't have words for how I feel.

I had several roommates—another revolving door—but I liked the last one. Raised in a middle-class African American family, she was the only adopted child among her siblings. She married for love, and on her wedding day, she realized she had made the mistake of her life. For the whole first dance he didn't look at me once, she said; he looked into every guest's face to make sure they knew it was his show.

By the time she told me this story, her husband was confined to bed and blind from diabetes. She took care of him along with a nurse. She watched TCM with him because he remembered the exchanges in old movies. Still, she said she was angry because everything in their life was about him.

Have you ever thought of leaving him? I asked.

She said she had throughout the marriage, but she would not. I don't want my children to grow up and think a man can be abandoned in that state, she said.

Yet she had tried to kill herself—an attempted abandonment of both her husband and her children. But this I did not say because it was exactly what many people would say to a situation like that. One has to have a solid self to be selfish.

19.

There is this emptiness in me. All the things in the world are not enough to drown out the voice of this emptiness that says: you are nothing.

This emptiness does not claim the past because it is always here. It does not have to claim the future as it blocks out the future. It is either a dictator or the closest friend I have ever had. Some days I battle it until we both fall down like injured animals. That is when I wonder: What if I become less than nothing when I get rid of this emptiness? What if this emptiness is what keeps me going?

20.

One day my roommate said she noticed I became quiet if she talked about Buddhism with me. I don't mean it as a religion, she said; for instance, you can try to meditate.

I did not explain that I had read Buddhist scriptures from the ages of twelve to twenty-three. For the longest time they offered the most comforting words. The teaching of nothingness diluted the intensity of that emptiness.

My father taught me meditation when I was eleven. Imagine a bucket between your open arms, he told me, and asked me to listen to the dripping of the water into the bucket and, when it was full, water dripping out from the bottom. "From empty to full, and from full to empty," he underlined the words in a book for me. "Life before birth is a dream, life after death is another dream. What comes between is only a mirage of the dreams."

21.

My father is the most fatalistic person I have ever known. He once admitted that he had not felt a day of peace in his marriage and expressed his regret that he had never thought of protecting my sister and me from our mother, who is a family despot, unpredictable in both her callousness and her vulnerability.

But the truth is, he tried to instill this fatalism in us because it was our only protection. For years I have been hiding behind that: being addicted to fatalism can make one look calm, capable, even happy.

22.

For a while I read Katherine Mansfield's notebooks to distract myself. "Dear friend, from my life I write to you in your life," she wrote in an entry. I cried when I read the line. It reminds me of the boy from years ago who could not stop sending the designs of his dreams in his letters. It reminds me too why I do not want to stop writing. The books one writes—past and present and future—are they not trying to say the same thing: *Dear friend, from my life I write to you in your life?* What a long way it is from one life to another, yet why write if not for that distance, if things can be let go, every before replaced by an after.

23.

It's not fatalism that makes one lose hope, I now understand. It's one's rebellion against fatalism; it's wanting to have one's time back from fatalism. A fatalistic person cannot be a dreamer, which I still want to become one day.

24.

"The train stopped. When a train stops in the open country between two stations it is impossible not to put one's head out of the window and see what's up," Mansfield wrote at the end of her life. This is the inevitability of life.

The train, for reasons unknown to us, always stops between a past and a future, both making this *now* look as though it is nowhere. But it is this nowhereness that one has to make use of. One looks out the window: the rice paddies and alfalfa fields have long been the past, replaced by vineyards and almond groves. One has made it this far; perhaps this is enough of a reason to journey on.

Amongst People

A heat wave was general all over Ireland the day I arrived in County Leitrim. Everyone I encountered—the border control officer, the woman who drove me across the country from Dublin, the hotel receptionist who handed me a bronze key with gold tassels—commented on the extraordinary weather. Shortly after I checked in, a county councilman and a photographer met me in the lobby, and they too started talking about the heat wave.

Children, unlike their elders, do not converse about weather. It is a fact to them, connected to the present only. Is it because weather can represent too much that it is often reduced to small talk? Weather gives experiences a place in time: a mood in which to inset a memory, a variable or a constant when comparing now and then. Two days later there would be a wedding at the hotel. Lucky bride, people said, as the good weather held, and I could see that it would be reminisced about for years to come.

In a corner store the photographer, a man in his sixties, asked for a betting ticket and three ice cream cones. I tried to decline, but he wouldn't allow it—the ice cream cones were the best and only a euro each, he said. We then climbed over a brick wall that guarded a private dock. *No trespassing,* a sign warned. I want you to look as though you're carried away by your reading, the photographer said, directing my position, legs dangling over the water, a book open in my lap, for which the ice cream cone was neglected. Now turn to me and smile, I want County Leitrim to see how happy our guest is. It was late May, and the ice cream melted fast. I watched it drip onto the wooden planks. Weather not forgotten is that which is lived through with effort.

Afterward I took a walk through town, past a few pubs, a florist's, a betting shop painted blue. There were not many people in the street. Eventually I came to a local attraction the photographer and the councilman had insisted I visit. It was the smallest chapel in Ireland and said to be the second smallest in the world. Nevertheless, it had all the solemnity I imagined: stone facade, stained glass, marble altar, iron gate. The chapel was built for a Mary Costello by her husband after her death, and later he was laid to rest next to her. The thick opaque glass covering the two coffins was an unsettling yellow, and in between there was enough space for a visitor to turn around. I lingered because there was no other place I wanted to go in town, and I had been advised to avoid the isolation of my hotel room and seek out even the most basic human interactions.

My mind was in poor shape. The week before there had been the thought of admitting myself to a hospital, but Ireland had seemed more sensible. I traveled often during this time, as with every trip, there was the hope of returning a different person. Amid the unraveling I did not foresee the peril of misjudgment. The week after Ireland would end in an emergency room.

On the layover in the Amsterdam airport, I had caught a glimpse of myself unconscious on the floor of a freight elevator, the door of which had been left open. The thought was a comfort. One could die on a trip. I had been keeping a journal. If my mind was losing control, I wanted it to be a process that could be understood by words, but I did not record this moment in Amsterdam. I did not understand, nor did I want to, the encounter in the airport. The journal was—and remains—a long argument with myself: a lucid voice questioning judiciously, and a more forceful voice speaking defiantly, sometimes in reply, other times in digression. The experience is like a confrontation between George Eliot and Dostoyevsky. The former counsels self-restraint through self-improvement, and the latter interrupts with monologues on impassioned and imprisoned souls; when the latter strives to be coherent or even sincere, the effort, under the gaze of the former, seems ludicrous. One always knows how best to sabotage one's own life.

Can one live without what one cannot have—the question appeared repeatedly in my journal. To say no was to give in; to say yes was surrender, too, though masked as bravado. What is it that cannot be had—this I avoided putting into words. Any explanation would be too specific and too small. But the understanding was never far from me.

Against my intuition I have formed attachments—to a few people, to a profession, to an adopted language—but I have yet to learn to live with them. Instead, the pain of being close to another person and the pain of isolation invalidate each other. To be able to write and to write in English are a lifeline, and a lifeline must be dismissed as extraneous, even illicit. Again and again my mind breaks at the same spot as though it is a fracture that never fully heals: I fear taking you—you, my life, and all that makes it worth living—seriously.

In Leitrim I did not run into the phantom seen in Amsterdam. Outside a bookshop I read a poster advertising a symposium on Rūmī. A laundromat had a handwritten note taped to the door, saying it would stay open only three days a week due to the recession. In the hotel lounge I sat with a pot of tea and counted passersby. A woman who reminded me of a friend prompted me to look up the name of an island off the coast of County Mayo, where her father had been buried on a rainy day, the coffin lowered into a foot of water. The tangible often possesses a kind of eloquence. Distractions bring momentary clarity.

THE TRIP WAS for a festival celebrating the Irish writer John McGahern. When the invitation came I could not claim much connection beyond admiration, but I wanted to visit the River Shannon and the country lanes in Leitrim and Roscommon. To see the setting of an autobiographical author is to hold fleetingly another person's reality.

I am not an autobiographical writer—one cannot be without a solid and explicable self—and read all autobiographical writers with the same curiosity. What kind of life permits a person the right to become his own subject?

Though I had read McGahern's memoir before, and knew that it would not provide an answer, I brought it for the trip. A painful childhood, losing his mother at a young age, growing up under a violent and volatile father, his exile from Ireland and his return—all of this he writes about plainly, showing off none of the literary ventriloquism of many of his countrymen. No one's vulnerability is more devastating than the next person's, no one's joy more deserving. What happens to McGahern is only life, which happens to us all.

Harder to endure than fresh pain is pain that has already been endured: a reminder that one is not far from who one was. Why write to open old wounds. Why relive a memoir, when that too is an indulgence.

. . .

A WORD I hate to use in English is *I*. It is a melodramatic word. In Chinese, a language less grammatically strict, one can construct a sentence with an implied subject pronoun and skip that embarrassing *I*, or else replace it with *we*. Living is not an original business.

Certainly in every era there are visionaries and revolutionaries and eccentrics, but they, conscious of—or, even more predictable, living for—their images, tend to be tedious. Stripped of audience, originality would be much less at ease with itself.

To bear the lack of originality: even the least ambitious among us have to invent some way to believe we are distinctive and irreplaceable. One wonders if this desire, humble and presumptuous though innately human, gives the permission for the use of *I*. Yet for months after the hospital stays I tried to explain to those around me that anyone can be, and should be, replaceable. What does this *I* matter to *you* when it means so little to myself?

In the aftermath of the Tiananmen Square massacre, the entering class of our university was sent to the army for a year to prevent future insubordination. In the army, with youthful conceit, I presented myself as someone different from others: submitting obliquely subversive poetry when I was ordered to write propaganda, making cleverly insolent comments about the officers, taking every opportunity to undermine the authority of our squad leader. To defy any political authority, to endanger myself in a righteous way, to use my words to distinguish this self from people around me—these, at eighteen, were shortcuts to what I really wanted: confirmation that life, bleak and unjust, was not worth living.

Before we left the army the squad leader wrote to me (it was a tradition to write farewell notes to one another): "Some people are commonplace, others are not. A day spent with the latter leaves enough memory, more than years spent with the former. As an ordinary person, I count it as my luck to have spent a year with you."

She had been raised in a military family, deferential to anyone superior, genuinely believing in the power bestowed on her by the army, trusting Communist teachings (how I had made her suffer and rage by insisting on talking about the Tiananmen massacre).

The note was written without malice, but it mortified me. I always feel grateful to her for letting me see how tedious a person can be when striving to impress the world with personality. It's fortunate, too, that my boringness was shown to me in such a gentle manner. Had she seen through me and written out of sarcasm, I might have become defensive about my foolishness. But she was too young to realize she was more real than the poseur I had become, and I was not experienced enough to feel guilt. A person, by dismissing her own self with a morbid carelessness, could easily bulldoze another person's beliefs.

. . .

A FEW MONTHS after the Leitrim trip, when I was in the hospital for a second time, I had a roommate with the bluest eyes I have ever seen. She asked me whether she should go to another facility or stay there. I didn't understand her question, and she rephrased it: Should she be cured of her disorder before going to rehab, or the other way around? I had no professional opinion but ventured to say perhaps it was not a bad thing to be drug free. You don't understand, she said, and explained that she would use drugs until she died.

I didn't know what else to say so I listened. She talked—about her childhood; the New York City subway; friends she had grown up with, none of whom acknowledged her existence now; her father and brothers, who had refused to loan her money; the halfway house that had let her down. Soon I had to excuse myself from the room. She was too insistent in demanding an answer. I was sad to lose the seclusion, however limited, behind a half-closed door. Your roommate, several women said to me, eyeing her torn paper gown and oblivious half-nakedness when she moved about in the hallway, where we all sat on sofas or chairs, socializing as we had been encouraged to do.

In a conversation with my new roommate after the old one had been transferred, I said something in a harsh tone that I had heard others use. You can't talk about her that way; she's like you and me; she's ill, my new roommate said, which stunned me. I had not thought of myself as ill, but stranded.

Seneca, writing about his "frailty" when spending time with people, stated that "there is not one of them that will not make some vice or other attractive." (I am fond of Seneca and his disciple Montaigne. Their wisdom and their self-assurance go so closely hand in hand that one feels an urge to poke fun at them while admiring them.) If I replace *vice* with *language,* though, it describes an experience I know well. I am easily influenced by people's ways of talking—their words, intonations, and quirks.

In the army a blurrily photocopied edition of *Gone with the Wind* circulated among my peers. More than half the girls in my platoon—their personalities ranging from shy to chatty to outright mean—claimed they saw themselves in Scarlett O'Hara. Some of the girls were too interesting, others too boring, to be Scarlett. This collective longing must be part of self-making. There is little originality in this process; all the same, what a brave thing it is to do.

I did not see myself in Scarlett O'Hara; or Anna Karenina or Tess Durbeyfield or Jane Eyre; nor did I look for myself in Jean-Christophe or Nick Adams or Paul Morel or the old man fighting the sea. To read oneself into another person's tale is the opposite of how and why I read. To read is to be with people who, unlike those around one, do not notice one's existence.

There was a girl in the army who had a few times stolen yams or buns from the mess hall for me. The gesture, which I did not know how to decline, filled me with cold resentment. To be thus singled out means one has to acknowledge a status the giver awards herself; worse than to be beholden to someone is to be beholden for things one does not want. In the hospital, three women made a game of smuggling oranges out of the dining room into my drawer. That I ate oranges like a good, sane person amused them as much as the Tolstoy novel and the Montaigne essays—I had asked for them when a friend visited—I carried around. I accepted the contraband fruit and welcomed their jokes, though I quoted a Graham Greene character—a Catholic priest—saying they could laugh at me but not my books. One of them would be transferred to rehab; the second, having failed other treatments, was to start ECT; the third was placed on suicide watch the day before my departure. One must laugh at oneself with those who are in situations not much different from one's own.

The hospital reminded me of the army. Habitat-specific vocabularies form a prism through which the civilian world looks fantastical; jokes are shared property; one's mind becomes a boundless maze, a compensation for the unavailability of physical space; to be seen by all is the easiest way to hide; to speak, and to speak someone else's language, the best mode of silence. How can the world at large be any different?

. . .

THE FIRST EVENING in Ireland I took a walk by the
Shannon. Other than a lone fisherman and a moored
boat, there were few reminders of the human world. Were
the waterbirds, the reeds, the falling dusk, and the foreign
sky enough proof that life was worth living? Across the
river were hilly meadows, and beyond, the lanes McGahern wrote about.

> A maze of lanes link the houses that are scattered
> sparsely about these fields, and the lanes wander into
> one another like streams until they reach some main
> road. These narrow lanes are still in use. In places,
> the hedges that grow on the high banks along the
> lanes are so wild that the trees join and tangle above
> them to form a roof, and in the full leaf of summer it
> is like walking through a green tunnel pierced by
> vivid pinpoints of light. . . .
>
> There are many such lanes all around where I live,
> and in certain rare moments over the years while
> walking in these lanes I have come into an extraordi-
> nary sense of security, a deep peace, in which I feel
> that I can live for ever.

I underlined the words "an extraordinary sense of security, a deep peace" and then did something violent: I
hurled the pen into the water. It sank soundlessly, and I
regretted the action right away. I had never in my life

harmed or destroyed an object out of uncontrollable emotions: not a door slammed, not a plate or a cup smashed, not a piece of paper torn into pieces. I must have inherited this respect for things from my father, who is a hoarder, though I have resisted forming an attachment to any object, or any place. I wished then and I wish now that I had never formed an attachment to anyone in the world either. I would be all kindness. I would not have done anything ruinous. I would never have to ask that question—when will I ever be good enough for you?—because by abolishing *you,* the opposite of *I,* I could erase that troublesome *I* from my narrative, too.

I stayed by the river until it was too dark to read on. The wounds McGahern reopened in his memoir are not the kind to be healed, forgotten, or worn as a badge of honor through hardship; in laying them bare (yet not raw), he seems to acknowledge that he misses the good things taken from him and wants them back. There is no greed in this wanting—greed comes from lack and a desire to be rid of it by any means. He is at peace with wanting. Perhaps this is why the memoir is always difficult for me to read. If there are things lacking in my life—and there are, as is the case for everyone—I have resolved never to want them. This must be greed too; wanting nothing is as extreme as wanting everything.

The lanes described in his memoir—with flowers that never failed to blossom, with siblings and a mother who walked together day after day before illness and death disrupted them—are not so different from the paths I had known in Beijing. Garden Road was an asphalt road with ditches on both sides that flooded when it rained. There was no garden along the way, only wild grapes and Xanthium bushes and weeds known to me not by their names but by their changes through the seasons. It was safe as long as a child did not stray, and once, when my father was away for a nuclear test, my sister, five and a half then, walked forty-five minutes to where Garden Road joined a bigger street and shopped for vegetables. The path I took to the elementary school circled our apartment block, behind each window some grown-up keen to catch a child in a bad deed; cut through an open field where we hunted grasshoppers in summer; passed a scantily roofed outhouse—muddy on rainy days, fly-ridden in dry weather—which served the school as well as a nearby People's Commune; and had a most threatening stretch— out of anyone's sight, no longer than a hundred meters— between the outhouse and the school. In first grade my best friend and I were accosted there by a man with a knife on a winter afternoon, but we were able to escape, screaming all the way back to the school to alert the teachers. In fourth grade, when the friendship was no longer sturdy enough for us to walk home together, my friend was seized by another man with a knife and taken behind the outhouse, a misfortune much talked about, but the harm could not be undone, so nothing was ever done.

There must have been plenty of times when I had someone next to me on those paths. Before my friend and I drifted apart, we invented games to play on the way to and from school. Once my sister and I walked the entire distance of Garden Road to see a movie, a school event, to save the bus fare. We left an hour early and every ten minutes or so waved at a passing bus when our class-mates called out to us. Once my grandfather—my moth-er's father, who lived with us—took me to a district post office beyond Garden Road. He gave me a grand tour, including a counter where packages bundled in old pil-lowcases were examined and then sewn back together by an old woman in a green uniform. He also composed a message, on a card with green grids, to demonstrate how to send a telegram. ALL IS WELL DO NOT WORRY, it said, and was delivered to a telegrapher behind a pane, and a few minutes later a receipt was brought back, promising the telegram's arrival later that evening. It was dispatched to a niece of my grandfather's whom he had not been in touch with for twenty years.

These moments shared with others—to write about them is to revive feelings, but it is to leave those feelings behind that I write. It is the moments spent alone that are the preferred narrative: I was happy walking by myself. It did not matter that there were men lurking behind the outhouse or exposing themselves with one hand while steering a bike with the other; older boys waiting to ambush me with rocks; a mean girl from my sister's class who followed me with a list of insulting names she rotated daily (Meatball was one, Bighead Carp another). These moments were not forgotten because they formed the background of aloneness, which was an intensely gratifying experience. There was, I remember, a brick wall around a nursery school next to our apartment building, and I would circle the wall for a long time, poking at the centers of the bricks, convinced that in time each brick would bear a dent left by my finger, of the same shape and at the same height.

Willfulness is a strange optimist. It turns the inevitable into the desirable. If aloneness is inevitable, I want to believe that aloneness is what I have desired because it is happiness itself. It must be a miscomprehension—though I have been unwilling to give it up—that one's life could be lived as a series of solitary moments. In between, time spent with other people is the time to prepare for their disappearance. That there is an opposite perspective I can only understand theoretically. The time line is also a repetition of one's lapse into isolation. It's not others who vanish, but from others one vanishes.

Willfulness is also a pessimist. It turns the undesired into the inevitable. The unhappiness I knew well—my mother's shrill, my father's reticent, my sister's bitter—was to be endured as weather or national politics. Did we ever ask ourselves: Why are we so lonely, so proud, and so adamant about perfecting our pretense? We kept our secrets well, from the world and from ourselves, and out of fatalism we cultivated stoicism. For years I refused to see our unhesitating compliance with my mother's behavior, not even when she announced, on the day I got married, that I had left her with only the hope for my divorce. It's one of those moments that one repeats to oneself and others as a joke, along with the tale that the Johnson County judge who married us at a brief ceremony, in front of an American flag and the state flag of Iowa, with two friends as witnesses, later had an affair with the assistant district attorney, a scandal where scandals are scarce. Laughter, however inadequate, insulates one.

SOME OF MY earliest literary education came from a set of illustrated autobiographies of Maxim Gorky. The three palm-sized books—*My Childhood, In the World, My Universities*—abridged and supplemented with vivid ink drawings, were called *little people's books,* though they were not for children. (It was a literary format that had made Shen Congwen, one of my favorite Chinese writers, lament the loss of literature in Communist China— even an illiterate person could flip through them, just as I started reading the Gorky autobiographies before I had learned any Chinese characters.) As a child, though, I obtained endless pleasure from these three books—my own possessions, and I owned very little. There was not a sin-

gle dull page: Gorky's grandfather beating his grandmother, his stepfather kicking his mother, his uncles
convincing a kindhearted young man to carry a heavy
cross to the graveyard and watching him get crushed to
death without any remorse, Gorky being clubbed as an
apprentice. Death happened every few pages: his father,
his brother, his mother, a young man with consumption
who used to hum melancholy tunes, friends and neigh-
bors and strangers. The book's messages—hardship, in-
equality, Gorky's political awakening—all these were lost
on me. What entertained me were the range of characters:
ragpickers, rich relatives, sailors, townspeople, priests,
icon painters, shop owners, longshoremen, widows, pros-
titutes, beggars, a one-armed man, a blind man, a cook
who cried over the beauty of poetry, a beautiful woman
who loaned Gorky books, a tyrannical bakery owner
mourning his pigs poisoned by his hired hand. (What a
strange introduction to Russian literature. Beginning with
Gorky feels like climbing on top of a bungalow, not real-
izing that nearby lies the Great Wall of China.)

Rereading the autobiographies now, I can still recognize the allure of the books. Gorky goes through a life
that maims and defeats others but always leaves him center stage, more elevated and heroic and charismatic with
each adventure. There is no time to be wasted between
one drama and the next; in fact, there is no life to be lived
between dramas.

The time between dramas: Gorky happily edits out that space from his life; McGahern seems to find peace in that space for living and writing. I would be livid if I took Gorky's position; I admire McGahern's without understanding it.

WHAT IS PEACE, what is security? All I wish, when bleakness besets me again, is to be left alone, to curl up, and to stay still. I cried when I reread the ending of McGahern's memoir the other day, with his mother and the lanes they had loved:

> If we could walk together through those summer lanes, with their banks of wild flowers that "cast a spell," we probably would not be able to speak, though I would want to tell her all the local news.
>
> We would leave the lanes and I would take her by the beaten path the otter takes under the thick hedges between the lakes. At the lake's edge I would show her the green lawns speckled with fish bones and blue crayfish shells where the otter feeds and trains her young. The otter whistles down the waters for the male when she wants to mate and chases him back again to his own waters when his work is done; unlike the dear swans that paddle side by side and take turns on their high nest deep within the reeds. Above the lake we would follow the enormous

sky until it reaches the low mountains where her life began.

I wish I had left a part of me on those walks in China, and it could peek into this life and know that its resolve to stay a fugitive is wise. Instead, one holds on to smaller doses of that nowhereness: reading a book that keeps the world at bay for as long as the words last, making up stories about characters who care little about one.

I wonder if I am late in recognizing this: fatalism is not following the predestined path unquestioningly; it is at every turn making a defiant decision against one's intuition. The part that could be so free and happy on its own is not fit to live among people. It strives in vain to articulate its right to be; it shies away from drama or feeling yet the avoidance only leads to melodrama; it compromises one, it shames one, it terrorizes one; it makes one's life into a cautionary tale. But subtract it and one's life becomes another cautionary tale. A life lived to forget is a life lived to remember, too.

ON MY SECOND day in Leitrim, I was interviewed onstage. One of the few things I remember talking about was McGahern's country lanes that were still around, and the roads in Beijing that no longer remained. The auditorium, going up at a steep angle, was filled with readers who came back each year for the festival. When I described the places as McGahern described them, they murmured in consent. An old man said, the way you looked up when you talked, you reminded me of John. I was moved. There was no way for a Chinese woman to resemble an Irishman but for love and memory to say so.

After the interview, I met one of McGahern's sisters. I said something about his books, and the talk went back to the country lanes. I'll never forget them, I said.

And I'll never forget your chicks, she said, speaking of the excerpt from my novella "Kindness" that I had read earlier:

When I was five, a peddler came to our neighborhood one Sunday with a bamboo basket full of spring chicks. I was trailing behind my father for our weekly shopping of rationed food, and when the peddler put a chick in my palm, its small body soft and warm and shivering constantly, I cried before I could ask my father to buy it for me. We were not a rich family: My father worked as a janitor, and my mother, ill for as long as I could remember, did not work, and I learned early to count coins and small bills with my father before we set out to shop. It must have been a painful thing for those who knew our story to watch my father's distress, as two women offered to buy two chicks for me. My father, on the way home, warned me gently that the chicks were too young to last more than a day or two. I built a nest for the chicks out of a shoe box and ripped newspaper, and fed them

water-softened millet grains and a day later, when
they looked ill, aspirin dissolved in water. Two days
later they died, the one I named Dot and marked with
ink on his forehead the first to go, followed by Mush-
room. I stole two eggs from the kitchen when my father went to help a neighbor fix a leaking sink—my
mother was not often around in those days—and
cracked them carefully and washed away the yolks
and whites; but no matter how hard I tried I could
not fit the chicks back into the shells, and I can see, to
this day, the half shell on Dot's head, covering the ink
spot like a funny little hat.

I have learned, since then, that life is like that,
each day ending up like a chick refusing to be returned to the eggshell.

People often ask if the incident with the chicks happened to me. That I never answer the question is accepted
as a coy acknowledgment that the episode is autobiographical. But I have never had a chick in my life. I did
not desire, on those Sundays when I trailed behind my
father with the ration book, to own anything. There was
no outsider who knew our story. There was, however, a
woman who had once tried to talk with me as though I
were a grown-up. She was older than my parents, and I
did not understand her singling me out. She embarrassed
me. My mother and her friends laughed at the woman's

intention to start a friendship; I always crossed the street when I ran into her.

When one does not have to account for one's own existence in it, however, the world offers abundant joy. The co-op, with a cluster of shops around a courtyard, was a crowded place, but there were enough curious sights for me to endure the pushing and yelling and sometimes fist-fighting among strangers. At the general store, where I stood in a queue for soap and laundry detergent and matches and, rarely, half a kilo of animal crackers, there was an overhead transit system with motorized wires. The shop assistants attached the payments to the metal clips, the money traveled to the cashier, and the change and the receipt traveled back—how it happened so reliably I could not figure out. Behind another counter, a row of jars stood in line, arranged by size, the smallest one my height, each with an apparatus affixed to the top. When a customer handed a bottle to the assistant, he needed to raise a lever to release the right amount of liquid—soy sauce, vinegar, sesame oil, or cooking oil—into the bottle. The meat and fish department boasted the biggest cutting board, which traversed the entire shop. It was always cold and damp there, as it was always dry and warm where rice and flour and beans and cornmeal were sold. The last was my favorite stop, as my father would let me help him hold a cloth sack, its mouth snugly fit around a metal chute. When the assistant measured out the ration, she tipped over the metal pan, and with a dull puff and a cloud of fine dust the flour or the rice filled the bag, weighing down our hands.

To exist as fully as the world expects one to, yet to remain absent inwardly: not equipped with words to articulate the secret I nevertheless understood it at a formative age.

When I left the auditorium, I wondered when and where and how I had gone astray from that intuition. Why are we told to seek out people? In forming attachments, does one become more than oneself, or does one lose an essential means of preserving oneself? The danger of forming an attachment—to a person, to a place, to a profession, to a cause, even to one's own life—is that one can trick oneself into believing that an attachment has a reason, and worse, that the reason can be mistaken as a right.

WE GATHERED AT the dock, where we were to board a boat—*Moon River,* the boat I had seen the evening before—to the barracks at Cootehall, where McGahern grew up. His sister said farewell to us. Is she not going? I asked, and someone said that she had joined the excursion the first year of the festival, and it had proved too traumatic an experience after not having seen the barracks for decades.

The Shannon widened as we went westward. Across the river there was a beer garden; drinkers waved and their waves were returned. A small boat sped past us, pulling a young man on water skis, but before we had time to appreciate his skill, he lost his balance. His companions went on obliviously, and the young man laughed, bobbing up and down in the water. Farther downriver, on both banks there were brand-new houses that had been left unfinished, or, if finished, unoccupied. All over Ireland it was a sad sight, these mansions deserted. Sadder still was to see horses—status animals during the boom years—abandoned, skinny, roaming in the wilderness.

At Cootehall, and later, on the walk to Henry's Bar—places that appeared in McGahern's memoir—people came and talked with me. They pointed out the lanes, the buttercups blossoming in the evening sun; and at a cemetery, the graves of those said to be characters in McGahern's novels, including two of my favorites, *Amongst Women* and *By the Lake*. Many of the festival participants had known him in person; others had been his readers for years. An old woman who had traveled from England said that her father had grown up not far from Cootehall. A man told me about two locals arguing who between them was the real person behind a character. When he asked me if I ever put people I knew into my books I shook my head. Never, never, never, I said with a fake shudder, and he laughed.

Why write autobiographically? There must be a belief in some kind of freedom. For Gorky, the freedom seems to come from his ability to judge the world according to a system in which he holds a strong belief: right and wrong, good and bad, future and past, all presented in unmistakable contrast. For McGahern, who judges neither others (including his father) nor himself, what is the freedom? Though freedom, like originality, is curious only as a universal fantasy. How people endure the lack of freedom is more interesting to me than their pursuit of it. Besides, those who clamor for freedom, like those who pose for originality, can be rather predictable, too.

But for those who wish to erase their selves by writing: Why write at all? I was working on a novel, the writing of it so intertwined with the rapid unraveling that I had started to view the book—in which a murder, halfheartedly intended, takes place—as a haphazard murderer of many good things in my life. But that, I knew too well, was to find an excuse for a dilemma that I wasn't able to sort out. When I gave up science I had a blind confidence that in writing I could will myself into a nonentity. I had for a few years relished that status, living among the characters who did not know my existence. But how does one remain forever an emotional hanger-on when one wants the characters to live, if not better, or more honestly, or more wisely, at least more fully? Uncharitably one writes in order to stop oneself from feeling too much; uncharitably one writes to become closer to that feeling self.

It was crowded in Henry's Bar. Friends and acquaintances greeted one another. Drinks were passed over shoulders. After a while, when everyone was settled, people took the stage and read from McGahern's memoir, some from the book, others having memorized the text. The readers followed one after the other, and then, ever so naturally and without an introduction, McGahern's voice came in:

> In another week Mother came home. She was well and happy and went straight back to school. With her each morning we went up the cinder footpath to the little iron gate, past Brady's house and pool and the house where the old Mahon brothers lived, past the deep, dark quarry and across the railway bridge and up the hill by Mahon's shop to the school, and returned the same way in the evening. I am sure it is from those days that I take the belief that the best of life is life lived quietly, where nothing happens but our calm journey through the day, where change is imperceptible and the precious life is everything.

I must have been one of the few to have encountered that voice for the first time. The passage, which I had underlined many times in McGahern's memoir, is an epiphany that only the most confident dreamers dare to claim. Did I envy McGahern? At that moment, yes, because I wanted to trust his words, yet I knew I did not. I, too, could feign such truth: I had often glided through life with deceiving tranquility; I had the confidence to put up a seeming as my being. That confidence, however, is the void replacing *I*. The moment that *I* enters my narrative my confidence crumbles. Can one live without what one cannot have—the absence of *I*, and the closeness to people that makes that absence impossible?

THE NEXT DAY an Irish writer showed me around the countryside. We drove past an IRA memorial, and half a mile farther an old couple making turf—with the good weather, she said, they would have a productive day. In a castle hotel we visited the McGahern Library. A golden plaque had been dedicated by the former Irish prime minister Bertie Ahern, and his name was defaced. Unhappiness about his role in the collapse of the Irish economy, it was explained, which reminded me of a teacher in middle school who had been disliked for her tireless preaching in the Theory of Communism class, and someone had carved her name on an ancient pavilion pillar in the Old Summer Palace adjacent to campus, a vandalism that led to a police investigation. When the news spread we all went to visit the pavilion during lunch break. In every protester there is a heart capable of gleeful childishness.

We drove to see McGahern's grave, where he is buried next to his mother near a small white chapel. Behind his and his mother's stones there was a gate, which led to a shaded path and beyond, a handsome-looking house, half-hidden among well-groomed trees. I wondered if it was part of the church, and my guide said she thought not. Then it came back to me. When McGahern's mother died, his father drew a plan for the plot himself, though with a mistake it blocked a path from the family house of the Dolans, who had donated the land to the church and had the privilege to come through their private path rather than through the congregation's gates. Legal issues arose; the Dolans had to be appeased.

> I remember an old uncle of theirs vividly, Charlie Dolan, who had spent years in America and was fond of fishing. Most days in summer he passed our house in Corramahon on his way to and from Garradice. Whenever he caught a big fish he hung it from the handlebars of the bicycle even though the tail trailed in the dust and the body of the fish slapped awkwardly against his knee as he cycled along. . . . It was a childish world. People knew his weakness . . . and Charlie was stopped at every turn of the road. The huge fish was admired in wonderment: it must have taken a near miracle to get such a monster up on the shore, and Charlie never failed to rise to the bait. This need for recognition and glory must have its roots in human loneliness.

To recognize the path and the house and the story behind it—it was the closest to clarity I felt on that trip. Not peace, but solidity. An unmistakable event from someone else's life had left unequivocal evidence. McGahern's life was lived among his people, his books written among his people. His characters, real and fictional, are no better and no worse than their creator, who—again unlike many of his brilliant countrymen—wastes no time in seeking originality. "The people and the language and landscape where I had grown up were like my breathing," McGahern wrote toward the end of his memoir. It is only natural to return to the memories. There is relief in redrawing the boundary between suffering and feeling; there is joy, too.

The paths I walked by myself in Beijing are gone. Even if the city had remained unchanged, I have turned away from the people and the language and the landscape. Homecoming, in my case, would only be meaningful followed by leave-taking. A permanent homecoming would be a resignation. To be among people—does that require one to be at home with others, to be at peace with oneself? But an agitated mind does not know any road to peace except the one away from home, which time and again exposes one to that lifelong phobia of attachment, just as to write betrays one's instinct to curl up and hide. Every word one says, every word one writes, every dream and fear and hope and despair one reveals to others and to oneself—they all end up like chicks refusing to be returned to the eggshell.

Memory Is a Melodrama from Which No One Is Exempt

One of the most callous criticisms of Stefan Zweig's suicide along with his wife Lotte came from Thomas Mann. "He can't have killed himself out of grief, let alone desperation. His suicide note is quite inadequate. What on earth does he mean with the reconstruction of life that he found so difficult? The fair sex must have something to do with it, a scandal in the offing?"

Death, except for someone entirely isolated, is always a personal moment made public. Suicide, among the most private decisions one can make, is often taken over by the public. Those who express strong feelings mistake themselves as the center of a story. The intense emotions around suicide—anger, pity, unforgivingness, even condemnation—demand what no one has the right to claim: an explanation, and the authority to judge the explanation.

One's wish to die can be as blind and intuitive as one's will to live, yet the latter is never questioned. A suicide can be dismissed as a drama gone awry and entering the realm of melodrama. If a tragedy makes us weep out of compassion and a comedy makes us laugh out of appreciation, a melodrama alienates and discomfits. When we cry, we cry under protest, suspicious of being manipulated; when we laugh, we laugh with the belief—doubtful—that we are beyond its absurdity. But this is a misunderstanding of melodrama. Tragedy and comedy involve an audience, so they must give—sharing themselves to elicit tears and laughter. Melodrama is not such a strategist. It meets no one's expectation but its internal need to feel.

My intention is not to defend suicide. I might have done so at other times in my life, but I have arrived at a point where defending and disputing my actions are the same argument. Everything I say is scrutinized by myself, not only the words and their logic but also my motives. As a body suffers from an autoimmune disease, my mind targets every feeling and thought it creates; a self dissecting itself finds little repose.

In the ideal, argument is a commitment—both parties, by giving and taking, discover something new. But this belief is as naïve as a young person's idea about the perfection of love. The possessiveness in human nature turns loving or arguing into something entirely different: winning, conquering, owning, destroying.

The talent of argument becomes about finding the right rivals—those who can be awed or bullied into agreement—and dismissing those who cannot be as irrelevant. That talent needs an audience. The world will always quote Mann on Zweig's death. Yet the latter's silence prevails.

There is another way to cope with the same auto-immune condition. A friend is good at arguing against herself from the perspective of others, even when she sees through the fallacy of their arguments. The mind, to avoid targeting itself, becomes two: one which, by aligning with others, is protected; and one which, by staying quiet, eludes being conquered. A self preserved by restraint is the self that will prevail.

MY SISTER HAD a classmate in college who was afflicted with lupus. She seemed sanguine about dying young, and indeed she had less than two years to live. Lying on her bunk bed in the dorm, she would talk about her boyfriend, who worked as a bodyguard for a wealthy family in Hong Kong, and the expensive dresses he bought her, which she was planning to distribute to her friends and classmates upon her death. When I read Elizabeth Bowen's biography, I recognized the young woman's impertinence in Bowen's mother. When she was diagnosed with cancer in her forties, she talked cheerfully about her imminent death, only months away. The first time I met William Trevor, he told me where he would be buried. I visited the seaside Irish town the next summer. The trip was not made for sentimental reasons. I am still not much different from the person who watched unblinkingly the young woman in Beijing when she talked about the dresses that would outlast her. I have always believed that, between living and dying, from being to being no longer, there are secrets understood by those nearer death. I want to know them, too.

But knowing is not understanding. There is a moment in the hospital that I return to, when a nurse chased me down the hallway because I could not sit through a morning meeting where everyone was to state an achievable goal for the day. She was a stern-looking woman, slim built with hair dyed platinum. You have to understand, she said, a suicide attempt is selfish. Someone close to me said it was irresponsible; another said manipulative. Yes, I know what you mean, I said to each of them. Understanding cannot be willed into existence. Without understanding one should not talk about feeling. One does not have the capacity to feel another person's feelings fully—a fact of life, democratic to all, except when someone takes advantage of this fact to form a judgment. One never kills oneself from knowledge or understanding, but always out of feelings.

IN LIFE WE shun melodrama, as its audience and, more urgently, as participants. In its original meaning, melodrama was the music that accompanied speech or pantomime onstage. Its purpose continues to be to evoke feelings rather than to narrate plot or create characters. But feelings carry value like currency. People like to think they have control over their feelings in connection with others. I feel for you, I'm happy for you, I'm angry on your behalf, people say; or else they say, You don't deserve my love, sympathy, respect, or hatred. These words reflect a status. Those who feel can stop doing so if they want; and they will, if their expectations are not met.

When I was in the army—and for a time was in despair—I felt the only solution for life was the trigger of a machine gun. I could not bring myself to do it—though this could be a lie of memory, a revision to avoid other truths—because I was aware two people, whom I knew little, would have their careers and perhaps even lives destroyed by my action. The platoon leader and the training officer, who supervised the shooting drill, were both kind to me. They would not have had any idea of the melodrama playing out in my head. I can see clearly how I appeared to the world. My glasses had been broken in a combat drill, so I had to borrow a pair from a chemistry student for shooting practice. Her right lens had a similar prescription to mine, but the left lens was much stronger. At the range I would drape a handkerchief in front of my left eye to save myself from disorientation. A piratess, I remember laughing with a friend.

After I left the hospital for the second time, I attended two days of volunteer training at a hospice service—to sit with the dying, as that was the only task legally allowed for a volunteer. Many speakers came: doctors, nurses, social workers, office managers, a spiritual healer, a chaplain, veteran volunteers, family members. My favorite speaker was a former ballet dancer, who started his talk with a song, the lyrics taken from an Emily Dickinson poem; when he finished singing, his pink shirt was drenched with sweat, and he left the audience in tears. My least favorite was the woman who ran the volunteer program. She was newly married and spent the time before the training and during the breaks showing a slideshow of her wedding and honeymoon. Isn't he handsome? she asked, insisting on confirmation from the room. She also pointed out an old friend of the bridegroom, who, drunk before the ceremony ended, had cut and stolen a piece of her wedding cake. She made it clear to this man to stay away from the marriage.

Both tragedy and comedy allow us to experience solid emotions, which are possible to share. Sorrow becomes less excruciating, laughter more resonant. Melodrama puts us on guard. We are the uneasy enemies of our own melodramas as much as other people's.

JUNE 2014. As I write today, the world is inundated with images of and opinions on the Tiananmen Square massacre from twenty-five years ago. Everything is said with certainty. People, especially those watching a tragedy from afar, talk with such eloquence. Anger, grief, idolization, and idealization of a historical event full of discrepancies, untrustworthy characters calculating on both sides with people's lives as betting chips, farces even—these feelings are readily expressed with an arrogance similar to Mann's. Those who speak without understanding have no trouble finding center stage.

When I was reading the news earlier, a random memory, which I had forgotten, returned to me. My sister was in medical school then, and went with her classmates to Tiananmen Square to help the students on hunger strike. From one of the visits she brought back a sun hat for me. Made of thin white muslin and shaped like a Victorian bonnet, it was called a Jane Eyre hat, and I had always wanted one. After the massacre, the hat vanished. No doubt my father, who had gone to a nearby hospital to count bodies the day after the bloodshed, was the one to have purged it. As an item donated to the protest it might incriminate my sister.

Melodrama is that Jane Eyre hat. To make sense of the memory I would have to go through decades of history; I would have to intrude into other people's pasts. Nevertheless it would be a futile effort. I could parse tragedy and comedy on all levels—national and familial and personal—yet the Jane Eyre hat would remain elusive. I would never be able to explain why its memory made me weep.

That flimsy object could be turned into something more than it was—a symbol or a metaphor; it would become much less than what it was. Melodrama, stubborn, refuses such transformation.

. . .

To ARGUE FOR and against melodrama, as with suicide, is to argue against myself. As one in the audience, I have been suspicious. I have occupied melodrama, too. Yet this experience is what makes me not dismiss melodrama. To understand it, I offer this hypothesis: memory is melodrama; melodrama preserves memory.

Memory is a collection of moments rearranged—recollected—to create a narrative. Moments, defined by a tangible space, are like sculptures and paintings. But moments are also individual notes of music; none will hold still forever. In the instant they are swept up in time—in that shift from space to time, memory is melodrama.

Yet melodrama has not much chance to survive. Not brave enough in that instant, we miss the music and are left to replace it with interpretation. If we do capture the music we regret the action—it is hard to live with melodrama. Time brings an audience—external critics and censoring self, adept at tainting, diminishing, or even erasing the melodrama. But time, that fatal enemy of memory, presents itself as an ally when memory agrees to be excised and spliced into optimized existence. The music turns less unbearable, more fragmented; what remains is an altered score.

In the end, memory has two forms, neither exempt from distortion: as melodrama and as adaptation. One holds on to the latter so the former does not make a shipwreck of one's mind. Shorn of the melodrama, though, what does one have but an empty life of busyness?

ON SEPTEMBER 18, 1940, the SS *City of Benares,* a British ship heading to Canada, was attacked by a German U-boat. The passengers included ninety children, and seventy-seven of them were lost. This ended the British government's wartime evacuation of children overseas. Not on the ship and thus not lost was Eva Altmann, age eleven, who had at about the same time boarded another ship that was headed to New York. Eva was the niece of Lotte Zweig. By then the Zweigs—having been uprooted by the Nazis and having migrated from Austria to England to New York and eventually to Brazil—had settled in Petrópolis, where they would live until they committed suicide two years later.

The Zweigs—who had arranged the papers for Eva's travel and secured a host family for her ("you may be both sure that we will look after her and bring her back grown-up and perhaps with a Yankee-accent," Stefan wrote to her parents)—received cables informing them of Eva's safe arrival just before the news of the SS *City of Benares* reached them. "The shock of reading in the paper the news of the disaster, was as great for us as it was for you, and I can understand how you feel about it," Lotte wrote to her brother and sister-in-law. "That thought haunted us for days. Fortunately your cable had arrived the night before. . . . Well, at least she is safe . . ."

That thought was unspecified in the letter—the descent into hell does not have to be imagined fully. Lotte moved on to describe the exotic, peaceful landscape of Petrópolis. *Well, at least she is safe.* The sentence, both candid and off-putting, stood out when I read the letter. This was between the two hospital stays; I often saw in people's efforts to make someone feel better a dismissal.

The sentiment expressed in that phrase, *well, at least,* is familiar, in wartime as well as in everyday life. Around the same time as the sinking of the SS *City of Benares,* a mother in Shanghai lost her young son to diphtheria. *Well, at least,* no doubt people pointed out—if they took the trouble to console her—she had two older children, and a new one on the way.

A glimpse into the depth of other people's misfortunes makes us cling to the hope that suffering is measurable. There are more sorrowful sorrows, more despondent despondencies. When we recognize another's suffering, we cannot avoid confronting our own, from which we escape to the thought of measurability. *Well, at least,* we emphasize. Our capacity to console extends only to what we can do to console ourselves.

The Zweigs' letters were written in English. The recipients—Lotte's brother, sister-in-law, and mother—lived in England then, and letters in German would have been checked more closely. To read Stefan's letters in the original language appeals to me, as I have only read his books in translation. To read Lotte's words is important, too; after all, she made the decision to end her life at a rather young age.

Their letters from Brazil, especially the later ones, are shrouded in melancholy. Toward the end of their lives, several times Lotte describes how they sit on their front steps between eleven and noon, watching, often in vain, for the postman to bring letters from Europe and America. "We have the impression to be still more away from you than ever," Stefan wrote. Waiting is treacherous. Rather than destroying one with the clean stroke of catastrophe, it erodes the foundation of hope. "We are looking every days [*sic*] through all the newspapers for good news," Stefan wrote around the time when he was arranging for Eva's travel. The next year, working on a biography of Montaigne he would not finish, he wrote: "It is good to read Montaigne in these days and all those who give good lessons in resignation."

In resigning, Stefan gave up belief in measurability—there is no hierarchy in suffering. In the South American letters, he often reminds himself that his position—away from the war and with a place to write—is to be envied. But how do we compare the despair of Stefan Zweig—who attended a carnival in Rio a few days before his death and expressed his "mixed feelings to assist to [*sic*] such fantastic explosion of joy in a time where nearly in the whole world explosions kill people"—to the despair of a fifteen-year-old in China, who, seeing little hope in a life trapped in a village, drank weed killer? Her last days were photographed by the media, from a girl on a stretcher to a body wrapped up in a plastic sheet.

"There is in reality not much to tell as our private life is of no importance now and the public events have enough publicity," Stefan Zweig wrote on December 31, 1941. To take one's private suffering into one's own hands: Is it not a rebellion, too, a refusal to have one's life measured against other lives?

A FEW DAYS before the anniversary of the Tiananmen massacre, I was interviewed on a radio program. It was meant to be about books, but for a while I was asked to recall how the protest in April progressed to bloodshed in June. Surely someone could have done the research beforehand, a friend said afterward. No, it's not about research, I replied; it's about having a historical event placed in a personal tale. In the following days I refused several interview requests. "All that I can say has been said," I wrote in my last email. "I hope you understand that I have nothing more to add."

The truth is, my impatience comes from the fact that what can be said, on a radio program or on TV, is always a simplification or a distortion. The desire for an individual's experience to be connected to something larger comes from both the audience and the actor, and the performance is evaluated by its relevance to the time. One either has to submit oneself to that script, or else choose to only speak on one's own terms.

In any interview it is impossible to talk about the Jane Eyre hat. There are other memories that cannot be told. When we returned to school a week after the bloodshed, a friend who lived near the square made us laugh with all sorts of tales. The least harmful one was about her uncle, who would open a can of Coca-Cola when her grandparents were not paying attention. Coca-Cola, or any soft drink, was a rarity at the time, and the popping would make the old couple jump from nervousness as gunshots had. Was it cruel of us to laugh? After that summer she left the country to join her parents in Germany, and later sent us a package with chocolates and a cassette tape, on which she had recorded stories about her new life. Three of us listened to her monologue, of accidentally locking herself in the wrong restroom at the airport, of stepping into dog waste while ogling an apple on a pushcart, of going to school without knowing any German (her parents had arranged for her to attend night school in Beijing to learn German, but she had either skipped classes or brought trashy romance novels instead).

When it was our turn to record a cassette to send her, we stalled. Beijing was the same city, windy and dusty on that November evening; high school was the same place, some classmates asked about her news, others had already forgotten her. The summer before, with martial law enforced, the four of us used to ride bicycles to a post where a soldier who had a crush on her was stationed with his troop. When he got a half-hour leave, we stood at a street corner, watching our friend lecture him about the evildoing of the People's Liberation Army. The boy soldier, not yet twenty and with a red face, pleaded with her not to endanger herself. Martial law continued into the next year, but after her departure we did not revisit the post. Unable to find stories to make our friend laugh, we ate the chocolates and never sent her anything we had intended to.

I HAVE, FROM an early age, been familiar with one person's memory. When she was born, her mother, having lost a son to diphtheria, had already gone mad. The girl took care of her mother between ages ten and eighteen, while her father and her older siblings pursued their careers elsewhere. During those years there was a young love, a student who had to drop out of nursing school because of tuberculosis. He rented a room across the courtyard from the mother and daughter. The scene—her sitting in front of her window, halfheartedly doing her schoolwork while he rests his arms on his windowsill and talks with her—this scene had been described to me many times. It is so familiar it may as well have come from a Zweig story. One has no trouble understanding it. The girl loses her mother, who dies in an asylum; the girl also loses the young man to an early death. But external misfortune—illness, epidemic, war, natural disaster—is not melodrama. Melodrama is absolute loyalty to the original moment.

It has been pointed out by some critics that my fiction is not political enough. A young man confronted me at a reading, questioning my disinterest in being a political writer. A journalist in China told me that most writers believe in their historical responsibility toward our time. Why can't you live up to that expectation? they ask, and my reply, if I were to give one, is this: I have spent much of my life turning away from the scripts given to me, in China and in America; my refusal to be defined by the will of others is my one and only political statement.

Melodrama is never political. It's not my responsibility to manipulate the memories of my characters. It is presumptuous of anyone, other than the characters themselves, to label their experience, or to impose meanings upon their memories. Characters who do so have agendas, yet they are not my agenda. My curiosity is to watch how memory, both as melodrama and as controlled narrative, lives on in time. Who among us dares to assert that our memories are not tainted by time, sweetest poison and bitterest antidote, untrustworthy ally and reliable annihilator?

SOMETIMES I IMAGINE that writing is a survey I carry out, asking everyone I encounter, in reality or in fiction: How much of your life is lived to be known by others? To be understood? How much of your life is lived to know and understand others? But like all surveys the questions are simplifications. How much does one trust others to be known, to be understood; how much does one believe in the possibilities of one person's knowing and understanding another.

In life we seek like-minded people despite—or because of—the limit of knowing and understanding. We do so to feel less lonely, though it brings a different kind of loneliness. In seeking others, inevitably we try to control an interaction. We insist on being known only as the version we prefer to attach to ourselves. A narrative catering to others is not far from memories revised for ourselves: both move us away from the quicksand of feelings. And those who do know us beyond our chosen version—by proximity, by intuition, by observation—must provoke similar discomfort in us as melodrama does. Does our wariness of melodrama contribute to our wish to escape their eyes, or is it the other way around, that in avoiding meeting those who have more access to our interior world than we are willing to allow, we can feel momentarily protected from our own memories?

Much of life's complication is that in many important relationships, one becomes more than one. A child, running along the street to search for her mad mother mocked by strangers, is also the mother's guardian. A father, speaking of death as a relief, unknowingly becomes a coconspirator when the child has already found solace in the same thought. In friendships and loves beyond childhood—do they happen by luck or by will?—in these relationships, we choose to present more than one self, and with these multiple versions are memories suitable for one version but not the other. With these conflicted memories, relationships take on an unexpected element of melodrama, as none of the controlled narratives stay unchallenged. Shared memory could become shunned; though oftentimes it is shunned memory that connects one to another.

Only in the most extraneous or contract-bound interactions is there the possibility that each person takes up only one role agreed upon, and in these situations memory can be overwritten. One may also have a less complicated relationship with a book. The book is timeless; one has only to account for one's own changing in time.

To be more than one, to be several, and to live with the consequence, is inevitable. One can err the opposite way, and the belief in being nothing used to seem to me the most logical way to live. Being nothing is being invisible and replaceable; being nothing to others means remaining everything to oneself. Being nothing is one way to battle the autoimmune condition of the mind, and this is closest to my friend's silence. Yet silence is not melodrama, or at least it is not presenting itself to be.

STEFAN ZWEIG HAS been rediscovered in America in recent years, but to me he is associated with the 1980s, when I read him tirelessly as a teenager. In one of my favorite novellas, "Letter from an Unknown Woman," the recipient of the letter, a famous writer and womanizer, does not recognize the sender, a woman who claims to have loved him all her life. She was his neighbor as a young girl and watched him live a busy life among women. Later, he mistook her for a prostitute. She bears his child, who dies in the flu epidemic of 1918; she, about to die herself, writes the letter to narrate her lifelong love.

It is a melodramatic story in the sense in which *melodrama* is commonly used—it is not surprising that it has been adapted into films in several languages—but Zweig elevates the woman from a mere cliché by granting her a fate that most dare not meet. She does not deceive herself by finding dignity in her despair. "Such purposeless affliction," she says of her life, yet without regret.

When I first read the novella at fourteen, I was enamored of the woman's valiant loyalty. I now see what I missed. Rather than a story of unrequited love, it is a story about melodrama's transgression. The woman accuses the man of "almost inhuman forgetfulness," yet the necessity to forget is only human. What is truly inhuman is the woman's refusal. She has the courage to keep her melodrama intact; the callousness to imprison another person in it. This is the cruelty of melodrama—like suicide, it neither doubts nor justifies its right to be.

More damaging than becoming a victim of political or historical turmoil is becoming the casualty of someone else's memory. At the end of the novella, the man shudders. Who, then, lives in a real sorrow: the woman, who has maintained melodrama as the only form of her memory, or the man, who has been, and will always be, imprisoned by another person's remembering?

I am unfairly prejudiced against the woman because, unlike at sixteen, I am wary of the damage a person's memory can do. Do you know the moment I die your father will marry someone else? my mother used to whisper to me when I was little. Do you know I cannot die because I don't want you to live under a stepmother? Or else she would be taken over by an inexplicable rage, saying that I, the only person she loved, deserved the ugliest death because I did not love her enough. Why did you curse me so, Mother; why did you not stop her cursing, Father? Though the truth is, I do not want to know the answers. I resent even thinking about the questions—what others and the world have done should not define one as much as what one has done to oneself.

There is a defiance that comes only with youth and inexperience, the refusal to accept life as it is. In his memoir *Ways of Escape,* Graham Greene reminisces about the first film he saw at six—a silent film about a kitchen maid turned queen—and the music offscreen. "Her march was accompanied by an old lady on a piano, but the tock-tock-tock of untuned wires stayed in my memory when other melodies faded. . . . That was the kind of book I always wanted to write: the high romantic tale, capturing us in youth with hopes that prove illusions, to which we return again in age in order to escape the sad reality." Greene is the only writer I have read who acknowledges that he not only enjoys melodramas, but also wants to write them. *Me, too!* I wrote in the margin. It is the only time I have admitted my ambition, albeit to a dead man. It does not matter that I may fall short. To capture a moment—of life, of history—is less a reason to write than to return to confront the melodrama, to understand how illusions beget illusions, memories eulogize memories.

Rereading the novella this time, I have forgotten—or refused to remember—what was the music I heard in the first place. I respect the woman for her unyielding belief in memory. How many of us dare to claim that? There are people we long to invite into our memories, people we long to invite us into theirs; people we strive to build memories with for the future. Yet in the end, there is something unbearable in that music. One may catch a few phrases now and then in solitude, one may allow oneself to hear its echo in a story or in a passing conversation, but to share that melodrama with another person or even to acknowledge it fully to oneself requires wisdom and courage.

AFTER BREECE D'J Pancake committed suicide, his mother asked James Alan McPherson to write a foreword for his collected stories. Pancake had studied with McPherson at the University of Virginia in the 1970s, and they had become friends. McPherson was my mentor at the Iowa Writers' Workshop.

Pancake had a habit of giving presents to everyone in

his life. "He loved to give but never learned to receive. He never felt worthy of a gift," his mother wrote in a letter to McPherson. McPherson, too, was generous with presents. One summer he gave every workshop student a toy mouse that sings and does kung fu; another summer he gave everyone a book (*Master and Man and Other Stories* by Tolstoy); there was a sophisticated clock, palm-sized and ornamented with figures, that he wrapped up unevenly for our elder son before his birth; there was a gift set of *Goodnight Moon* for our younger son, McPherson's namesake; there were beautifully sculpted plates and expensive chocolates for our family from Von Maur, a department store in Iowa City where a pianist in a long dress played Chopin in the afternoon to a near-empty store. When McPherson turned sixty, a friend and I arranged to meet a flower farmer, the husband of my former colleague, in a parking lot to buy sixty flowers. It was fall, late in the season, and the farmer was annoyed at the timing. If only you'd asked last week, he said; I had better flowers then. McPherson received the gift as generously as he always gave.

"I always thought that the gifts he gave were a way of keeping people away . . . of focusing their attention on the persona he had created out of the raw materials of his best traits," McPherson wrote about Pancake. It is difficult to read that sentence. Pancake's desire to always give is familiar to me, though I cannot give without questioning my motives. Does giving have to do with generosity, or with the selfish comfort it brings? The self-deception it offers, when the truth is one has little, or nothing, to give? If one keeps giving, will one be good enough to be loved one day?

Unlike the woman in Zweig's novella, Pancake did not let the melodrama in him transgress. He gave more than he had, more than he ought to, but he did not trap anyone. People who have not experienced a suicidal urge miss a crucial point. It is not that one wants to end one's life, but that the only way to end the pain—that eternal fight against one's melodrama so that it does not transgress—is to wipe out the body. I distrust judgments—Mann's or anyone's—on suicide. They are, in the end, judgments on feelings.

There was a young girl in the hospital, a college student, who cruised the hallway warning of an invasion by some strange technology. Her mind was so brilliant and knowledgeable, her words so full of humor and wisdom, her admonishment as musical as the refrain of a Greek chorus, that I often watched her with admiration. During visiting hours her mother was always there, and once she brought a friend who had grown up with the girl. The mother and daughter walked back and forth in the hallway, and the friend, a step behind, wept soundlessly without wiping away her tears.

In his foreword, McPherson admits to keeping a distance from Pancake at a late point in their friendship. He refused to open a package from Pancake for months, until the news of Pancake's death reached him. It contained a gift, as McPherson had guessed; it also contained a letter, in which Pancake said he was not waiting for a reply—such a statement always means the opposite. The understanding between two people, and the alienation because of it—the friendship between McPherson and Pancake upsets me. It is one person's melodrama avoiding another person's melodrama; it is silence that does not prevail.

Someone asked me why I do not worry about feeling exposed while writing. It should be the most natural question for me, yet it has never occurred to me to ask. To be exposed means that a stranger could learn something about me through reading my words and against my wish. Perhaps he could, and he would come to a conclusion, right or wrong, though what would that do but define me in external terms?

The external has a limited claim on understanding and feeling. I can never say that I understand my characters; I certainly have no right to say that I feel their feelings fully. Though if I know them, however limitedly, it is enough for me to want to know them more. What is a more secretive way to struggle than struggling along with people to whom I remain unknown and unseen? My melodrama would not transgress and cause any damage to the characters. In life I do not have that confidence.

Is there, I wonder, an endpoint to knowing—not that one has known everything, but that one knows enough. This ceaseless effort—I have seen this trait in my friend who argues against herself along with the world—protects one from melodrama, as understanding and feelings do not.

EVA ALTMANN STAYED in America until 1943, when she reunited with her parents in England and later became a medical doctor. Had she died crossing the Atlantic, she would have become a footnote in the personal history of the Zweigs and the national history of wartime England. The word *affiliation* shares an etymology with *filial*. It is a child's fortune that she is not merely defined by her affiliation with her parents, her heritage, memory and history that deny her an independent future.

Eva was a small part of the Zweigs' final years, but reading their letters, I could not avoid the futile question: What if it had been arranged for Eva to live with them? In their letters, they often questioned whether it would be better for her to join them in Brazil, but in almost every letter they tried to convince themselves and Eva's parents that New York was a more suitable place for a young girl. In his last letter to the Altmanns, written the day before the Zweigs' suicides (postmarked three days later, it was received, like the letter in Zweig's novella, after its author's death), Stefan wrote, "Had Lotte's health been better and had we could have [*sic*] Eva with us it would have had sense to continue . . ." Would a young life around have offered an anchor? Three months earlier the Zweigs had also considered, out of extreme isolation, adopting a puppy—"Only we fear to get attached if one day we should have to move or leave again."

A writer's letters and journals grant her a triumphant position, however illusory, against time's erosion. They also award a reader the flattering feeling of kinship. When Katherine Mansfield claimed in her journal that she loved Chekhov so much she wanted to adopt a Russian baby and name him Anton, her emotional transparency embarrassed me. I felt the urge to laugh because I was terrified to recognize even a residue of myself in her. It occurred to me much later that she was by then dying of tuberculosis, the same disease that led Chekhov to an early death. Our admiration and scrutiny of another person reflect what we love and hate to see in ourselves.

What do we gain from wanting to know a stranger's life? But when we read someone's private words, when we experience her most vulnerable moments with her, and when her words speak more eloquently of our feelings than we are able to, can we still call her a stranger? I have convinced myself that reading letters and journals is a way of having a conversation with those writers, but surely it is as glib as calling perusing the music score of a symphony the same as listening to it. A conversation requires more than scribbling in the margin.

Sometimes I suspect that I am drawn to those who don't converse with me because I have not outgrown a childish wish that they will teach me how to live. Or, a slightly more complicated version: I wish that they would teach one how to die. But their deaths can only be read in edited versions. Their letters and journals come to an end, artfully and artificially maneuvered by the editors. The last one collected in Hemingway's letters is to a nine-year-old boy, written three weeks before Hemingway's suicide, and the boy himself only lived another seven years. Turgenev, on his deathbed, wrote to his estranged friend Tolstoy: "I am really writing you, therefore, to tell you how happy I have been to be your contemporary, and to express to you my final, sincere request. My friend, return to literature!" Mansfield's last note, from an unfinished story, ends with an observation that only the dying Mansfield would make: "It was an exquisite day. It was one of those days so clear, so still, so silent you almost feel the earth itself has stopped in astonishment at its own beauty."

All people lie, in their writing as much as in their lives. It frustrates me that I hold on to an unrealistic belief: there is some irrefutable truth in each mind, and the truth is told without concealment or distortion in a letter or in a journal entry. My obligation is to look for that truth; finding it will offer me the certainty I don't have in me. With that certainty I will find a way to build a solid self. This burden I never take on while reading or writing fiction.

I read the Zweigs' letters from South America because I wanted to understand how they had descended into the darkest depression. But the story line—if it could be called a story line—of Eva became a counterpoint to that descent. It had moments of laughter, mundanity, even pettiness. The Zweigs' comments on Eva's host family were not always kind; her boarding school in upstate New York was looked at with European suspicion; her tardiness in correspondence was blamed on the American influence; there was a fear that her host family would never return her; and again and again there was discussion of arranging for Eva to go to Brazil. As their letters became increasingly melancholy, and as they—especially Stefan Zweig—increasingly refused to believe in any hope for themselves or for mankind, Eva was never included in that despair. This impunity is the same wishful thinking as when parents want to spare their children the difficulties they themselves have had to live through. Yet without that wishfulness, what are the parents doing but letting the melodrama of their own memories dictate the next generation's fate?

ONCE IN A while I get an email from someone I have met briefly. "You may not remember me," these emails often begin, the hope to be remembered expressed by the acceptance of having already been forgotten.

Sometimes out of mere mischief I reply with a detailed account of our encounter. People are joyfully surprised when they are remembered, but I have not been honest with them. There is a difference between being remembered and being caught by the mesh of one's mind.

Many years ago, a young man from a peasant family in south China left home to study theoretical physics at a university. He was the first one in his village to have graduated high school. His mother could only afford to buy him a pair of socks, and the villagers gathered their limited means to give him a suitcase. He traveled north with a pair of socks in an empty suitcase. When he arrived, the university provided him clothes and bedding, and at once he joined the martial arts team. He was not a physical man, but he would compete for the next four years so that he could have enough food.

Eventually the young man met and married the girl from the courtyard. He became a hoarder of things, she a hoarder of memories. *Well, at least,* we could say, nothing would be wasted or lost, and indeed nothing has been. I grew up with the dread of seeing piles of old newspapers collect dust and used matches put back into matchboxes. But more than that, I dreaded the memories that were not mine, yet were so adamant to be heard and remembered as the only memories that mattered.

What becomes of someone raised by parents who cannot part with their objects and memories? Tangible objects crystallize memories, too. I wonder if there is a similar melodrama in my father's clinging to small and used things as in my mother's unrestrained vulnerability and cruelty. Nothingness—holding on to nothing, retaining nothing—was a shelter from melodrama until it stopped being one.

I was in Iowa City to give a reading, and McPherson asked me to dinner at his house. He had laid out plates, silverware, new napkins, glasses, and wine on a coffee table, and had a friend bring in food from a restaurant. Over dinner he talked a lot about his life, some parts I had known, other parts I had heard from people around him. The conversation could have gone on forever, and I constantly watched the time. Before I left, he asked if I could come again the next day, and I said I couldn't because I had to fly to Chicago in the early morning.

That was when I saw his tears for the first time. I met McPherson during a phase of his life different from when Pancake had met him, and I had never tried to connect the person I knew to the writer at his prime. Once, when he loaned me a book, I saw on the last blank page scribbling of a conversation with Ralph Ellison. I did not ask him what it was he felt compelled to remember. Over the years I nagged at him about his health, and when he was in good humor he would behave like a chastised yet uncooperative child, yet I felt a distance between us. I used to explain to myself that it was a result of my shyness and his Southern manners—he always addressed me as Ms. Li. But I now suspect that I only pretended there was a distance the same way he refused to open the package from Pancake. I wanted to believe I knew McPherson enough through his work. When one understands another person, perhaps knowing no longer matters, or it matters too much for one to bear.

There was a moment at the dinner when I thought I could see many things that were yet to come: McPherson's future, the deterioration of his health, his loneliness, and his increasing silence; and my future, too. That McPherson is not widely known and is largely forgotten now is not surprising. He rebelled all his life against what others wanted to make him into—an obedient serf, a political warrior. His refusal would be a futile battle in any era and in any country.

When the future becomes memory prematurely, one feels unbalanced. I ran away that evening because I did not want McPherson to see my panic. The next day I called a friend and asked her how he lived without killing himself. It was a terrible question, but what I could not say at the time was this: How could one stop oneself from seeking solace in the peace brought by death? I had indulged that thought at dinner with McPherson, as I had at various times wished that relief for my father. What is more indefensible, to give up one's own life, or to give up hoping for one's loved one's?

It is difficult for anyone to watch someone close suffer. The grief comes from not understanding the pain, and from knowing that suffering, even when it ends, will live on as memory. A child does not, and should not, understand her parents' memories, yet this incomprehension does not offer exemption. The child in every one of us carries the burden of memory's melodrama, not only our own, but those before our time.

"Thing were not *supposed* to be this way," Ralph Ellison, wounded by his time, said to McPherson. McPherson must have said that to himself, too. Disappointment like that must have come from the hope to be understood. I have run away from it to my nothingness, my fatalism, and my insistence on being irrelevant. Yet I have not had a moment of hesitation to read Zweig or Mansfield or other writers. One is protected in these cases. Their memories will never become mine.

The inadequacy of writing is similar to that of connecting to another person. It is essential that a story allow its melodrama to meet the reader's, yet melodrama makes such encounters rare.

"Phil Ochs hanged himself. Breece Pancake shot himself. The rest of us, if we are lucky enough to be incapable of imagining such extreme acts of defiance, manage to endure," McPherson wrote toward the end of his foreword. Such kindness, one cannot help noticing; such a contrast to Mann's coldhearted judgment. I never asked McPherson whether the thought of suicide occurred to him. I never asked him how he managed to endure. But it doesn't matter: I have to live in my own cautionary tale. Some people seek victory in that tale, others escape, yet others peace. I still do not know what I want from mine, but one hopes that to accept not knowing, for the time being, is better than to accept nothing.

Two Lives

Until an interviewer asked me if there was a book that I had read too young and thereafter haunted me, I did not realize that I had never used the word *haunt,* a word I find claustrophobic and insincere. Nor did I know that the word *haunt* has a connection to home. Etymologically, it is from the Middle English *hauten* (to reside, inhabit, use, employ), from Old French *hanter* (to inhabit, frequent, resort to), from Old Norse *heimta* (to bring home, fetch). When we feel haunted, it is the pull of our old home we're experiencing, but a more upsetting possibility is that the past has become homeless, and we are offering it a place to inhabit in the present.

I told the interviewer there is a book I may have read too early, though I wouldn't call it haunting in any way.

A book I read too early: to answer that involves sorting through memories—one does it with a dread of inaccuracies. When I started middle school, my father began jogging early in the morning, leaving home before I left for the bus stop, no more than a few steps ahead of me. It has taken me thirty years of not remembering to understand what I had thought of as his exercise habit as a father's tact. At six thirty the road between our apartment and the bus stop was not the safest place for a child. He never hovered, but there were days when the bus was early, and he would be at the stop before me, holding the door so that the bus would not leave without me.

Twenty minutes into the ride, I changed route at another stop. Several schoolmates also waited for the bus there—a longer ride that brought us to the outskirts of the city, where our school had been built on the land of the Old Summer Palace, a place of ruin and wilderness at the time. During the first week of middle school, a girl and her father ran for a bus that was just pulling in. We all watched while the father, holding the door for the girl, hurried her on. Why didn't you take the bus, he asked afterward—none of us had moved. We looked at one another, and finally someone replied that it was the wrong one. Though bearing the same route number, it was the regional line, which would never get the girl to school.

Like the memory of my father's jogging, this incident only came back to me when I tried to answer the interviewer's question. I can, in retrospect, reconstruct the father's worry and guilt, his dismay at our inaction; I can question our silence, not out of malice or indifference, but the fear of drawing unnecessary attention to ourselves. We were transitioning out of childhood then. The world—and the world belongs largely to adults—is an untrustworthy place. To be caught by uncertainty is worse when noticed by others. But inevitably the moment comes when one has to differentiate oneself.

For me, it was when, a month into the school year, I was chosen as a librarian's assistant. Twice a week another student assistant and I stayed until five thirty, giving out books through a window to the many hands that fought to give us slips with Dewey numbers written on them (each student was allowed to put down five numbers at a time and was allowed to check out one book). After closing, we shelved the books, cleaned up the slips left on the floor, and then were allowed our privilege: we could check out two books.

I had not been in a library until then. My literary education had consisted of ancient Chinese poetry from my grandfather's bookshelf, which I had obsessively memorized, and novels, both Chinese novels and translations, serialized in newspapers, unreliably available because I could not get hold of the newspapers consistently. (I missed half of *Resurrection* because the second part was not serialized, a loss I took hard in third grade. I also missed a major part of *David Copperfield,* which I made up for by watching the British miniseries, newly introduced to China, at our neighbor's place—we didn't own a television set then.)

Within a few months, I had finished all the books on

the literature shelves (the 800s, as I began to think of them). They were of uneven quality, good only for the palate of a hungry mind. Not much is retained. In fact, I remember only two books.

The first is an eighteenth-century novel in verse, *The Tale of Renewed Connections* (the translation of the title, which is mine, does not catch its essence entirely, though I prefer it to the title of the TV adaptation, *Eternal Happiness*). The author, Chen Duansheng, was born to an affluent family of literary pedigree. She began to compose the book at seventeen or eighteen to entertain herself, her mother, and her sister, and within two years finished sixteen volumes. When her mother died, she stopped writing for ten years, and only resumed when her husband was exiled for a political reason. She died in her forties, leaving the novel unfinished. Two other authors—less talented, as I was quick to judge—wrote three more volumes. Except for the first reading, I always stopped at the end of volume seventeen. One ought to be loyal to whom one deems a friend on the page.

The book can be interpreted in many ways—progressive, visionary, revolutionary—but I was not concerned about such things at the time. What captured me was the never-ending drama. A daughter from a wealthy family dressed as a man so she could travel freely and receive a man's education; she befriended two young men, one the future emperor of China, the other her future fiancé. Entangled in the love triangle was the upheaval of the time. The heroine's father was persecuted by political enemies; in order to save him, she entered the civil service. Predictably she ranked number one in the Palace Examination, with the surprising consequence of being chosen to become an imperial son-in-law. Her bride turned out to be her long-lost friend, who had tried to kill herself out of heartbreak, and had been saved and adopted by the emperor's uncle and made into a princess.

I was twelve and was developing a melodramatic streak despite a reputation of being aloof and bookish. I copied and memorized passages from the book, quoting them to myself in all kinds of moods. I felt an acute loss at not being a contemporary of the poetess, as though it would have changed the course of the book's life, or, even, the poetess's life. It strikes me now that invisibility, a prerequisite for my tireless conversations with dead authors, is the opposite of what my younger self desired. This wish to find a place in an author's life and make a difference to a book's fate: it must have taken bravery and naïveté to trespass.

Any young mind has to fall in love with a book once to learn how to read. My infatuation, fortunately, was ended by another book, written, in contrast to Chen Duansheng's, at the end of the author's life. I wonder who purchased for the library the thin, stern-looking volume— *Prose Poems* by Ivan Turgenev. There was not another book that could match its quality, and it was so rarely requested that against the rules, I renewed it week after week. I did not know anything about Turgenev other than that he was Russian. There were only his words, about conversing skulls, meditative mountains, friends stabbing each other in the back, a woman standing poised before her execution, the author contemplating his own death, and fleeting moments of youth and happiness. I did not know the book had been written toward the end of his career, throughout which he had been criticized for betraying his country, his coolness toward the progressive and the revolutionary, and his insistence on being an apolitical writer.

My mind was porous then, so perhaps the encounter with Turgenev did take place too early. Or perhaps the encounter happened at exactly the right time, a floodgate installed to keep out hopes and wishes indiscriminatingly.

A FRIEND, WHO had called me every day while I was in the hospital, continued to call daily afterward. Sometimes I could say nothing, only weep. You must write, she said all the time. I can't, I said. Your characters deserve to live, she said. I don't care about them anymore, I said. But I still care about them, she said. This conversation repeated itself, and then one day she suggested that we read *Sense and Sensibility* together. A few days later, she sent a message quoting Elinor's plea to Marianne, who refused to be mitigated in her grief: *Exert yourself.*

Where does one find that self to exert? Only by excluding it did the meaning of exertion become clear to me. My life during this period, other than taking care of my family, was lived almost entirely in reading. I reread everything by Turgenev on my bookshelf: his novels and stories and prose poems and essays and letters, and two biographies, including one by V. S. Pritchett. (I have always been partial to novelists writing biographies— Pritchett, Stefan Zweig, Romain Rolland.) This concentrated reading caused a small shift in my mind. What that shift is, and whether it is real, remain to be confirmed by time, but it feels as though in my long acquaintanceship with Turgenev I have finally come to a place where I can see him as someone from the distant past, the past to which he belonged, and the past in which I read him—as a middle-school student in Beijing, and as a new immigrant to America.

Rereading his collected letters, I came across a wine stain from a meal eaten alone in an empty hotel restaurant in Vancouver. After the meal I rehearsed with a jazz group in a dark theater. I could not hear my voice at all while reading. When I finished, one of them played on a bamboo flute a slow tune: *If you miss the train I'm on, you will know that I am gone; you can hear the whistle blow a hundred miles.*

"Five Hundred Miles"—which I first heard in Beijing as a teenager, which a platoon mate played on a cheap wooden flute during a march across central China, which I listened to after coming back from the hospitals—the song, like these memories, like Turgenev's books, belongs to a distant past now.

"Oh, my dear Tolstoy, if you knew how difficult I find things and how sad I am! . . . May God spare you the feeling that life has passed by and at the same time has not begun yet," wrote Turgenev in a letter. He was forty. Much of his major work was yet to be written. His decades-long quarrel with Tolstoy had not yet begun (the following year he wrote to a friend: "I have closed all my accounts with Tolstoy; as a person he no longer exists for me"). In another five years he would meet Flaubert— a friendship, more a kinship, that would last seventeen years, until Flaubert's death.

It would have to be either arrogance or cowardice that made a man, intellectually active and physically fit, say that his life had ended. In *War and Peace*, Prince Andrei, after losing his first wife in childbirth, "thought over his whole life and reached the same old comforting and hope-less conclusion, that there was no need for him to start anything, that he had to live out his life without doing evil, without anxiety, and without wishing for anything." He was thirty-one and had not met Natasha, the true love of his life.

It is not an unfamiliar story. What Turgenev bemoaned throughout his youth and middle age—that life had passed without having begun—was precisely what I had needed to hear when I first encountered him in the school library. All children require a system to stop being children. Fatalism beyond questioning became for me that system. There was the solace in imagining myself back to the period of Chen Duansheng or Turgenev or all those who had come before me. There was the advantage in believing I was old already because it released me from having to be young. There was the possibility of death, which allowed one to bypass digressions into a life that had to be lived in detail. Pritchett called Turgenev's pessimism absolute. The absoluteness—whether it is pessimism or optimism or fatalism—is the most effective defense against what haunts one.

WHAT HAUNTS, BEFITTING the word's origin, is home. Varvara Petrovna, Turgenev's mother, reigned over the household with pride and rage. His father, like the father in *First Love*, married for pecuniary gain, was unfaithful in the marriage, and died young. Ivan Turgenev was the younger of two sons and his mother's favorite. When his brother, Nikolai, married against their mother's wish, she cut him off and let him struggle on a clerk's salary to support his wife and three children. After years of effort on Ivan's part to reconcile his brother and mother, she arranged for the grandchildren to be brought out to the street in St. Petersburg, looked at them, and left. When the three children died in the same year she remained indifferent to Nikolai's loss.

Worse than enduring a tyrannical parent is to be the

favored child. I wonder if, even for the most uncharitable parent, there is a child whose role is to be the chosen one, and to be beaten when he cannot return the love at a reciprocal level. Varvara Petrovna loved Ivan with a vengeful and violent passion. "I alone conceived you," she wrote to him when he traveled abroad. "You are an egoist of egoist. I know your character better than you know yourself. . . . I prophesy that you will not be loved by your wife."

Turgenev lived most of his adult life abroad, an abandoner in his mother's eyes as well as in the eyes of many of his countrymen. But how else can one live with what haunts one? I don't even need to lay my eyes on you to know everything about you because you came from my body, my mother often said when I was growing up.

I SHIVER WHEN reading about a mother full of wrathful and possessive love. The thought that not all mothers are like that more and more is becoming a solace to me. There was Chen Duansheng's mother, who raised her two daughters as poets at a time when education was considered damaging to feminine virtue. It was reassuring to see that John McGahern was buried next to his mother. When I met a friend's parents, despite my theoretical understanding, it was extraordinary to see them interact with natural closeness. The fact that I had found it extraordinary made me cry afterward.

But one cannot have a different biography. One cannot find consolation in revision. One cannot relive age twelve to unread Turgenev. On the phone my father suggested, with a quantum physicist's mystic illogic and a fatalist's pure logic, that our difficulties be put into a new light. Who knows what we did in our past lives to others, he said; what we have is what we deserve.

How do we live with what we have, unhaunted? During the rioting of the Paris Commune, Turgenev wrote to Flaubert: "Oh, we have hard times to live through, those of us who are *born spectators*." But people are not born spectators—they choose to be. It is a decision made for the sake of living.

Turgenev never married. He spent much of his life in love with Pauline Viardot, a leading opera singer of the time ("that ugly Gypsy," deplored his mother), arranging his time—from Paris to Baden to London and back to Paris—to be close to her. He became friends with her husband and collaborated with him on translation projects. He asked the couple to adopt his illegitimate daughter and renamed her Paulinette after Pauline. When Pauline's stage career ended and she turned to composing operettas, Turgenev provided libretti.

Turgenev's talent was as a witness. His letters to Pauline and Flaubert included accounts of historical and everyday events. Writing from Paris about the revolution of 1848, he observed: "I was also struck by the way the hot-chocolate and cigar vendors moved around the ranks of the crowd. Greedy, pleased, and unconcerned, they

had the look of fishermen hauling in a heavily laden net."
On July 7, 1865, a scorching day in Washington, D.C., the
hanging of Mary Surratt, Lewis Powell, David Herold,
and George Atzerodt—conspirators in Abraham Lincoln's
assassination—drew crowds, and a reporter similarly noticed that "outside the prison, a different atmosphere pre-
vailed. Cake and lemonade vendors were happily selling
their wares." With the security of distance, life can be
looked at with curiosity—such is the comfort of a spectator.

FOR MANY YEARS I carried with me William Trevor's
Two Lives, a collection of two novellas, "Reading Turgenev" and "My House in Umbria," the former my favorite work by Trevor. In their fictional reality the two
protagonists have little in common: a Protestant Irishwoman from a small town who has chosen to spend more
than thirty years in an asylum; and an Englishwoman with
a handsome house in Umbria, a dubious past, and a shadowy present. A meeting between them would be unlikely.
That Turgenev would be read and memorized by an
Irishwoman in an asylum is not far from his being singled
out in a middle-school library in Beijing. One could easily
give meaning to the serendipity of reencountering him in
Trevor's work, though to do so is foolish. Connections
can always be created, an artificial system of symbols and
patterns. But life, which defies interpretation, eludes cliché.
I stopped carrying *Two Lives* with me after the hospi-

tal stays. I can't explain why. I was reading only dead authors at the time. Perhaps it was to resist medical advice and to isolate myself further. I distrusted all things solid in my life then. One afternoon, I sat on a bench with my younger son, waiting for his brother to come out of a class. We were not talking, as often we do not, but I was aware of his comfort in putting his hand in mine and keeping it there as though it was the most natural thing in the world. It must be, but it occurred to me that I didn't understand it. I could approximate understanding, but it would be only that of an anthropologist.

To PLACE TWO writers together because of similar details in their biographies reveals one's motivations and limitations.

Turgenev is mentioned a single time in Marianne Moore's letters. When she was eighteen, during a visit to New York City (a trip she called her "sojourn in the whale," her first contact with working artists and poets out in the world), she noticed his work next to Molière's in a bookcase at an artist's house. There is no reason to believe Turgenev's work mattered to Moore. One could imagine her disapproval of his indiscreet obsession with a married woman. One could imagine, too, his frustration with someone so impregnably upright. He would not have quarreled with her well, as he did with Tolstoy or Dostoyevsky.

I began to read Moore's letters after I saw, by chance, an often quoted line from her poem "Silence": "The deepest feeling always shows itself in silence; / not in silence, but restraint." I must have written something similar in Chinese in another life; in fact, I knew I had, and had lived as a subscriber to that belief. One makes oneself a rebel and a castaway simultaneously when renouncing a belief.

I was reading the letters and journals of several writers, and it did not matter to add another dead person. Their banalities, more than the brilliant thoughts and words, soothed me. Even the dullest entry or the most mundane correspondence pointed to an end. I have given up on many novels that bore me but I have never given up following a writer's journey in letters or journal midway.

Yet I did not find consolation in my own banalities. The days, slow because I was not writing, were measured by minutes, recorded in a journal because I wanted to understand how to exert oneself. An hour of weeping could be reduced to half an hour, to fifteen minutes; an undistracted reading of ten minutes could double or triple. Writing fiction is about understanding how time passes, years ago I had said to a friend. What I had not realized was that time could also stand still. Ten years passed in a few sentences for Maupassant's heroine. Yet to stay clear of any destructive impulse by keeping a deranged pen moving in the journal, I would often find, twenty pages later, that five minutes barely passed on the clock.

In a letter to a disheartened friend, Moore wrote:

> Whatever the problem, we must elude the sense of being trapped—even if all one can say to one's self is, "if not now, later." ... If nothing charms or sustains us (and we are getting food and fresh air) it is for us to say, "If not now, later" and not mope. I never fully succeed and am beginning to think I never shall; still, the automatic sense of participation, brings one along.

The automatic participation of life: I held on to that idea as a fake talisman. I did not believe that *later* would be any different from *now,* but I liked the sound of her phrase.

LIKE TURGENEV, MOORE never married. He considered marriage a catastrophe for art. Her poem "Marriage" opens by calling marriage "an institution" and "enterprise," but even earlier she had written, at twenty-four, in a letter to H.D.: "(There is no such thing as a prudent marriage;) marriage is a Crusade; there is always tragedy in it."

The parallel between the biographies of Moore and Turgenev is easily noticeable. Mary Warner, Moore's mother, separated from her husband shortly after Moore's birth, and he spent much of the rest of his life in a sanatorium for delusional monomania. Mary raised Moore and her older brother, Warner, by herself. Like Turgenev's brother, Warner married against their mother's wish. Unlike Varvara Petrovna and her infernal rage, Mary displayed enough magnanimity, though she was barely tolerant of her daughter-in-law. "My crime is that while I would count it nothing to die for you, I have refused to live for you," Warner wrote to his mother shortly after his marriage. Often I come back to that fortissimo line. Not everyone born to a tyrannical mother has the mental clarity and strength to articulate this decision.

I often contemplated Moore's words for days without fully grasping their meaning or why they felt so important. "Wilfulness in itself, is an attractive quality but wilfulness fails to take into account the question of attrition and attrition is inevitable," she wrote in a letter, which I sent to a friend. What did she mean? I asked.

Why do you read her in any case? the friend asked.

One reads and rereads writers with whom one feels kinship—Turgenev, for instance—or else those who, like D. H. Lawrence and Stefan Zweig and Romain Rolland, enter one's life at a particular moment and become part of personal history. Reading Moore, however, required a willfulness that matched hers. Not understanding, I could intrude only by continuing to read—a rebellion.

When I was ten, I set my heart on memorizing the great poets with the surname Li. There was the romantic craze for Li Po; the melancholy crooning of Li Yu, an emperor turned prisoner; Li Qingzhao, one of the few poetesses recorded in Chinese history who was not also a courtesan; Li Ye, a Taoist nun known for her amorous connections with several poets. And then there were two Tang dynasty poets I did not understand at all: Li Shangyin and Li He, both known for their allusiveness. What attracted me to their work, I now realize, was their unreadableness. Li Shangyin was meticulous with form, his meter and rhyme impeccable, his words painstakingly arranged, with splendid images and dense metaphors strung into indecipherable jewels; Li He was less constrained by form, but his poetry was equally obscure. It was a child's avenging joy to be able to quote—often only to myself—from the two poets whom even most adults around did not understand.

More experienced and less undaunted a reader, I wondered while reading Moore whether one has the right to claim a connection without understanding. Moore's letters are as perplexing as her poetry. Reading her is like trudging through a frozen snowfield in the dark. Even though her words seem to have been written out of the wish to communicate, together they take on a frustrating opaqueness. How can a person, writing in a genuine attempt to convey things that are important, make herself so unknowable? Moore's biographer—I did not read her book until after I finished the letters—mentions a similar frustration.

A writer's letters often exhibit a transparency, a naturalness even the most autobiographical work could not match. In a letter to Flaubert, who so rarely left his homestead, Turgenev wrote:

> Old age, my dear friend, is a great dull cloud that envelops the future, the present and even the past, which it makes more melancholy, covering our memories with fine cracks, like old porcelain. (I'm afraid I'm expressing myself badly, but never mind.) We must defend ourselves against this cloud! I think you don't do so enough. In fact I think a journey to Russia, the two of us together, would do you good.

Following the exhortation, Turgenev wrote about a four-day trip he had recently taken in Russia. The countryside in that letter was not much different from what was described in *Rudin* or *Fathers and Sons,* the observer's feelings having been felt by his characters. ("One comes out of it as if having been immersed in some sort of restorative bath. And then one gets on with everyday living again.") Still, to view it through Turgenev's eyes instead of his characters' eyes, to read him re-creating the scenery for the mind's eye of Flaubert, brings a strange satisfaction, not merely from eavesdropping. There is one more frame of seeing, the discrepancy between words written for anonymous others and words written for personal connections.

In his letters, Turgenev, forgoing his detached gaze at his characters, was prone to exaggeration and drama. Katherine Mansfield's cool, at times cruel, command in her short stories is a sharp contrast to the unrestrained wildness in her letters. Hemingway, exact in each word and its weight in his fiction, could be garrulous in his correspondence. (Once, entertained and annoyed by his repetitiveness on a small monetary matter, I wrote in the margin: *be Hemingway already!*) The contrast between writers' published work and private words makes one feel for them, but Moore's poetry and letters, equally opaque, close a door to anyone's curiosity. Perhaps my reading her is far from rebellion or intrusion. It is only to insist on being defeated. No one defeats better than Moore.

In a letter to her friend William Carlos Williams, which I reread often, Moore wrote:

The fact is, I must admit, that we usually exemplify— in some measure—the faults against which we inveigh. I am prone to excess, in art as in life, so that I resist anything which implies that the line of least resistance is normal. . . .

Make allowance, William, and muster charity. But no charity is needed so far as friendship is concerned, for friendship is my phobia. It is after all, loyalty which makes one resistful?

The letter says exactly what I am incapable of putting into words. To hear Moore say that she's prone to excess is not unlike reading young Turgenev's lament over being an old man before his time. Such absoluteness could be mistaken for affectation, but there are people who can survive only by going to the extreme.

A writer can deny she is autobiographical. But what is revealed and what is concealed expose equally. In that sense Moore, a master at withholding, is a highly autobiographical poet. I wonder how she would react to such an assessment. Were I told such a thing, I would recoil; I would put every word I have written up for examination to prove I have let nothing from my life slip through the cracks. Once—of all places in Beijing—a woman asked at an event if I was an autobiographical writer. No, I said, absolutely not. But your father is a nuclear physicist, she said, and in your collection at least two fathers worked in the nuclear industry. A coincidence, I tried to explain, does not mean a real connection, though my effort to disconnect writing from life, I now understand, is not different from Moore's excess. One writes about what haunts one. Thus looked at, no one is exempt from being autobiographical.

"I would have died long since if I did not excel at defaulting." Defaulting to what, Moore never said. Even when she did not refrain from talking about herself, it was abstract. If there is no proof of the existence of secrets, one is spared the fate of having two lives:

> one, open, seen and known by all who cared to know, full of relative truth and of relative falsehood, exactly like the lives of his friends and acquaintances; and another life running its course in secret. And through some strange, perhaps accidental, conjunction of circumstances, everything that was essential, of interest and of value to him, everything in which he was sincere and did not deceive himself, everything that made the kernel of his life, was hidden from other people. (Chekhov)

Marianne Moore reminds me of what I could have become.

OTHER THAN COLLEGE, Moore did not live apart from her mother until her death. When they first moved to New York City, a neighbor gave them a kitten, and they named him Buffalo. "Buffalo is developing and is cuter and cuter," Moore, deeply attached to the kitten, wrote to her brother. The next day, when she was at her library job, her mother killed Buffalo. "Mole [Moore's mother] got chloroform and a little box and prepared everything and did it while I was at the library on Monday. . . . And nothing could have been more exact. . . . But it's a knife in my heart, he was so affecting and scrupulous in his little scratchings and his attention to our requirements of him." Still, Moore could not but defend her mother. "It would have been cruel to him to let him grow and might have . . . seemed like murder to him if we *had* kept him and turned him over to strangers."

Together the mother and daughter let the Hudson River take the body away, and for a few years after they avoided the pier. The menacing logic by which Moore's mother functioned is familiar. When my sister started working after college, she gave me a pair of hamsters as a present. I became fond of them, and soon after they disappeared. I gave them away, my mother said; look how obsessed you are with them. You can't even show the same devotion to your parents.

Moore and her brother treated their mother as a child. I had known, long before I could put that thought into words, that the only child in our family was my mother. More than her rage I feared her tears.

My mother is a child I had to leave behind so as to have my own life. I admire Marianne Moore's brother. But sometimes action is propelled by hope that is only a wish; action does not absolve one's sin, action itself is the sin.

I remember those late winter evenings, after I served as the librarian's assistant, walking to the bus stop. Between the campus and the stop was a long avenue, unlit but for one lamp at each end. The campus was empty.

The Old Summer Palace, in those days, was a deserted place even during the daytime. The poplars flanking the avenue were black against the dusky sky, and the crows circled the treetop in their loud cacophony. Beyond the poplars were two narrow ponds. The lotus that had blossomed pink and white in the summer lay withered on the water's surface; nothing, I have always had the misimpression since then, can look deader than lotus in winter.

I would listen to my footsteps and recite Turgenev's words in my head, certain about one thing in that bleak moment. My father had told me, when I was five, that a person was in danger only when another person was around. When nobody was near me, I was safe; I could even imagine a different life. What I feared was arriving home. Too often my mother would be screaming at my sister; too often my mother would be crying because she was hurt by my father's defense of my sister. To be assigned as the one to smooth over her mood, to appease her anger, to bring her back to her childlike cheerful self so we could all breathe again—dreadful as it was, it was not the worst. This, I will tell you, was the worst—I shivered when I read that Moore's mother scrutinized not only everything Moore wrote, but her physical change day by day—too often my mother would question, with omniscient suspicion, if any man on the bus had touched me inappropriately. How could she not understand that I was made invisible by having been old already, too old for those men lurking in the dark?

. . .

"WE WRITE TO narrate, not to prove," Turgenev advised a young writer in a letter. I wish I had learned that earlier, though to prove, even as a failed effort, brings the relief of certainty, and what brings relief can become a habit, an addiction. The things I had wanted to prove were ambitious, even inhuman: to be free from all that haunts one, and to keep a distance so as never to haunt others.

I wonder if Moore wrote and lived to prove, and what she intended to prove, and to whom, and for what reason. Reading her makes me feel resentful: in her I see the self I wanted.

Turgenev was not afraid of showing his melodramatic nature (which must have matched his mother's—this possibility always disturbs me). Moore, whose melodrama was internalized to the point of annihilation, gave access to only one witness—herself. Unlike Turgenev, whom I now feel ready to leave on my bookshelf with other writers, Moore will haunt me for a long time—is it from understanding too little, or too much?

In never leaving home, Moore found a shortcut in suffering, and she suffered impeccably. "Writing, to me, is entrapped conversation," she wrote to Ezra Pound when he was in St. Elizabeths Hospital. I resent her for living an unhaunted life. I envy her for her entrapment. I can find no selfishness in her but her selfless art: sane, elegant, uncharitable.

Amongst Characters

I called my mother the other day and she reported that she was reading an old journal of mine. *At that very moment.* I changed the subject only to be guided back. She wanted to start keeping a journal and, looking for a suitable notebook, found one nearly unused, with only a few entries at the beginning. Written right after you left the army, she said. No, you don't have to read it to me, I said when she described the first entry. The paranoia I felt then is the same fear that has always been with me. Anyone reading one's words is able to take something from one. Had I been more disciplined I would have written nothing and lost nothing.

Philip Larkin, on his deathbed, asked that his diaries be destroyed. His request was carried out by Monica Jones—his longtime friend, intermittent lover, and later companion. Other private papers she allowed to be made public, a controversial outcome from a debatable will. At our first meeting William Trevor talked about one's wishes being misinterpreted, giving Larkin as an example. On that day I was aware that my understanding of Trevor's concern was hypothetical. I was thirty-four and he was seventy-nine; I had published one book, he, more than thirty. That one's words would be misinterpreted seemed to me as inevitable as death itself. What I did not know yet was that a young person's fatalism was only bravado.

When that bravado failed, fatalism became fatal. Or, to make a more honest statement: unless shut away in a journal that will be safely and timely burned, one's words will always be read, by design or by accident. Hiding behind those words is like entrusting one's self to a straw house—there is the wind, there is the wolf, and above all, there is one's urge to destroy the house before it is destroyed by an external force.

Between the two hospital stays, I was in London for a few days by myself. The hotel, a narrow house on a quiet street, had a strip of a garden guarded by high walls, and I spent much of the time there reading Katherine Mansfield's notebooks. When it rained I moved to the sitting room, which was hidden from the hotel entrance. Other guests appeared, but they were either too busy or too idle, and none of them seemed to be able to sit still for long. There were sights to see, and business to conduct. There was also time to kill. A woman picked up and put down a magazine without opening it; a son in his thirties walked into the garden once and again, bringing the same news

of rain to his mother; a man studied the marble fireplace
before his wife and daughters joined him.

To appear as the most idle person in the hotel—to not
have to venture out for business or sightseeing—and to be
able to sit still for hours: only in retrospect do I understand this extrication as a dangerous sign. It is an experience similar to when a child stares at something close
until he only sees nonexistent patterns—the mind makes
up what it wants to see.

Both busyness and idleness make people fidget. The
busy scatter themselves around, refusing to be occupied
by only one thing at a time; the idle are engaged with a
thousand trifles. The worst kind of fidgeting is that of
one's mind. In London, the more agitated I was internally,
the calmer I remained physically. I did not have to fight
the urge to turn a dark hotel room into a tomb as I had in
Ireland months earlier. The stillness I carried was enough
to make the world retreat.

That year I traveled frequently. In a hotel in Edin-
burgh, I sneaked into a medical conference and read the
posters about fractured bones and inflamed tendons,
imagining what might have been mine, a scientist's life
built on facts and diligence. In an Idaho homestead—
Ezra Pound's birthplace—where I was the only guest on
the second floor while the first floor serves as a museum,
I held still when visitors entered, fearful and yet curious
whether someone would lift the red velvet rope and walk
upstairs. It was the week immediately after the first hos-

pital stay, and against everyone's warning I had insisted on going to Hailey, where Pound started his life and near where Hemingway, seventy-six years later and ten miles away in Ketchum, ended his. At the airport in New York— returning from another trip to London—when the computer system crashed and trapped in line hundreds of immigrants, wary and patient, I entered the country with unquestioned ease, the first time I traveled with an American passport, a small gain in a year of ungraspable loss. Each trip had been meant to renew a belief that I had forgotten. *Nothing matters.* The belief was fallible, but I knew from experience that absence is more reliable than presence, and a lie sustains life with absoluteness that truth fails to offer.

MY FIRST YEAR in college, the university arranged for a reunion with the officers from the army. Our freshman advisor, who was male and thus not allowed to enter the female dorm, waited at the building entrance. When I did not present myself, he sent someone to fetch me, and I hid behind the curtain on the top bunk, refusing to respond to the knocking on the door. There was no reason to re-encounter the past, I rationalized; no reason to complicate a time line when it could be separated into terminable fragments.

Before graduating from college, a dorm mate asked me to sign a T-shirt that had collected many signatures already. I did what I was asked to, though I must have

shown reluctance, as my boyfriend—later my husband—
reproached me for my aloofness. But I don't see the point
of adding one more signature to the T-shirt, I said; in any
case she and I will probably never see each other again.

I believed at that moment I was speaking of a fact.
Was I speaking a genuine feeling? Perhaps only to the
extent that I wanted it to be true. The truth is, I knew
I would not forget the girl with the T-shirt because she,
like most people I have met, had qualities that made me
curious—in her case, it was the disarming way she mocked
her own mediocrity. I knew too I would not forget the
officers, who, without the army camp to grant them protection and authority, would only look inconsequential
and lost in Beijing. To remember is my instinct.

The possibility of being remembered, however, alarms
me—it is not from the wish for erasure, but the fear that
people's memories will erase something essential. Expectations met and unmet, interpretations sensible and skewed,
understanding granted or withheld, scrutiny out of kindness and malevolence—all these require one to actively ac-
commodate others' memories. Why not turn away from
such intricacy? The less I offer you something to remember, the better I can remember you.

The source of my difficulty, I had decided before I
went to London, was that I had gone astray from my belief. For years Tolstoy ended his journal each day with
three letters, initials for the Russian *if I live*. Every month
he began with the note *nearer to death*. How did I forget

to start each and every page of my journal with the reminder that nothing matters?

WHEN I WORKED as a researcher in a hospital laboratory, I studied asthma with mice as the animal model. My job was to inject ragweed into the mice over a period of time and measure the effectiveness of a new drug. There was a glass chamber where I put the mice to induce asthma and analyzed their breathing pattern. That and other data informed the progress of their illness, though imperceptible to me was how they felt individually. Suffering alone is not measurable.

The word *asthma* is from Greek, meaning "panting." But in ancient Rome, the doctors nicknamed it "rehearsing death." I took note of this detail while reading Seneca's letters. Seneca, like Dickens, Proust, Dylan Thomas, E. B. White, Elizabeth Bishop—the list could go on—was afflicted with asthma. (Lotte Zweig's unalleviated suffering from asthma was given by Stefan Zweig as one reason for her suicide.) Everyone, sooner or later, draws a last breath. Sometimes I think how tiring it is to read about artists with their mental illness. Wouldn't it be curious to study those who rehearse their deaths?

Elizabeth Bishop, on reading the death notice of Dylan Thomas, wrote to friends: "It must be true, but I still can't believe it. . . . Thomas's poetry is so narrow—just a straight conduit between birth & death, I suppose—with not much space for living in between." During the months bookended by the two hospital stays, in June and in October, I returned to that letter often. *A narrow conduit between birth and death*—I had always believed in the necessity of treating my life in the same manner. The space deprived oneself is allocated to one's characters; the excursions one takes with them, distractions and delays, are an antidote to impatience. You're impatient with yourself, with your work, with others, a friend said to me around this time; you're the most impatient person in the world.

Impatience is an impulse to alter or impose. Suicide is a kind of impatience people rarely understand, I replied to the friend, and quoted an Elizabeth Bishop letter in defense.

IN THE LAST year of high school I had the habit of playing truant, not worried about being caught. I was in charge of keeping attendance, trusted by the teachers, once in a while persuaded by my classmates away from accuracy. On one dreary winter afternoon, I skipped classes and walked in the run-down alleys near the school—now these alleys are lined with chic pubs and sophisticated eateries catering to expats and tourists. I was looking for a place I had read about in newspapers—the first and only one of its kind in the city, the article had said. This was before the time of telephones, and I did not have a map. It took me nearly two hours to find the place, a quadrangle among residential quadrangles, with more than ten plaques bearing the names of different organizations by the gate. I entered the courtyard and saw stacks of coal bricks piled up near one wall, several bicycles leaning against another. A woman came out of a door and asked me what I wanted. I'm looking for the Office of Volunteers for the Mental Health of the Next Generation, I said. The woman sighed heavily. I can't believe it, she said to someone inside; here's another one of those crazy kids. She then turned to me and said, They are not in today; go back and live your life, don't ever come here again.

The indifference of strangers is not far from that of characters, yet the latter do not make one feel exposed. They have no interest in interfering with my life; they have neither the time nor the curiosity to ask me questions; they do not preserve me in the amber of their memories. What else does one want from people but that kind of freedom—an existence closest to nonexistence?

The indifferent, though, have their powers. Again and again I let them usurp my dreams, and again and again they evict me from their world, oblivious of any attachment. *Now go back to your real life*—they dismiss me with the same words I used to end my phone calls to friends with, dismissing myself and masking it with lightheartedness. Do you, a friend asked me years ago, understand that you are in people's real lives? I remember feeling shocked—at the time, the only real people were my characters. When a book is finished, to mitigate the emptiness of their leave-taking, one kills them in a gentle manner—if there is any violence in imagining the action it is as secretive as a suicidal thought lodged in the corner of one's mind. Is writing not my way of rehearsing death?

I had gone to London with the thought of erasing a novel from the record, telling people it could not be finished and leaving the draft entombed in my computer. Not a rehearsal of death, but a clean severance. This novel had brought out of me unkindness against others and uncharitableness against myself. It had nearly derailed a friendship. It made me question which life—mine or the book's—mattered; perhaps neither did. Years earlier my husband had cautioned me that writing would require more than a scientific career. *No real madness, no real art,* he quoted an old Chinese saying, but I had refused to consider it an obstacle. If I had writing, what was there to fear?

Can one's life be at the mercy of one's characters? The possibility seems ludicrous, yet in my unraveling they were no longer my allies, confiscating from me the boundary I had so adamantly maintained between writing and the *rest* of living, which, I had believed until then, was to live minimally, to live but on the surface, to not live. One cannot sustain that kind of in-between—living and yet not living—forever. For the first time I wanted my life to be as legitimate as my characters', as solid, as habitable. Make me real, as you are to me—this cry could only be directed toward my characters. They were not meant to

see me; why then let the novel live on? I had refused realness to people in my life; why then let myself linger?

How could you have thought of suicide when you
have people you love? How could you have forgotten
those who love you? These questions were asked, again
and again. But love is the wrong thing to question. One
does not will oneself to love; one does not kill oneself
because one ceases to love. The difficulty is that love
erases: the more faded one becomes, the more easily one
loves.

My muddle, in retrospect, is clear: I had underesti-
mated my aversion to wanting anything; I had overesti-
mated my capacity to want nothing.

ONE AFTERNOON IN London I made a call to Trevor. He
told me about the spinal pains that had been afflicting
him. Don't waste your sympathy on me, he said; I'm an
old man. Then he asked about the novel. It's near finished, I lied, and he advocated for letting the work go and
not lingering.

The next day, I went to the British Museum, always a
trustworthy place to lose oneself among the living and the
long-gone. Afterward, in a bookshop not far from the
museum, I bought a copy of *Letters to Monica,* a selection of Philip Larkin's letters to Monica Jones, spanning
nearly forty years. As with Katherine Mansfield, whose
world I had entered with the simple goal of distracting
myself when I purchased her notebooks in a secondhand

bookstore, I picked up the letters because Larkin and Jones were irrelevant at that moment.

I sat in the bookshop café until closing time. In an early note Larkin compares a scathing letter from Jones to a letter, "charitably left unposted," from Mansfield to a young man named Frederick Goodyear. It starts with her telling Goodyear that he has misread her as a possible mistress, a few lines later lapses into an intimate and good-humored account of her day in a French villa, and ends with her request that he write again and signed, "With my 'strictly relative' love 'K.M.' "

Mansfield's letter would have been only a footnote to Larkin's correspondence—one underlines them all the time, thinking of looking them up later yet rarely doing so—except for the odd coincidence that I had read a draft of it the day before in Mansfield's journal. The language was so vehement that I had written in the margin, *What's going on?!* (The letter is also in Mansfield's *Selected Letters,* with no indication whether it was sent. Larkin's belief that it was charitably unposted is appealing.)

Unsent letters carry a kind of cruelty. A letter is written as a space shared by two people; by not sending it, its writer claims the power to include and exclude the recipient simultaneously. Out of cowardice or control an act is performed in the name of caring or discretion. Unsent letters should never be written. But what difference is there between an unsent and an unwritten letter? The truth is already there. Self-imposed silence speaks, too, though not to communicate but to punish.

IN THE SAME letter to Jones, in order to prove that he is not trustworthy, Larkin states that, rather than "a favorable image" constructed by her, he is more like "Portia's Eddie—or even Portia's father." Eddie and Portia and her father come from Elizabeth Bowen's novel *The Death of the Heart*. The reference was startling. The novel I was considering abandoning had been written in conversation with Bowen's novel. (One of the few fond memories about the ill-fated novel: I was in a basement in Los Angeles, talking with a radio interviewer, his eyes bloodshot from too much reading. I must ask this question before we go into the studio, he said, an old copy of *The Death of the Heart* in his hand; was this book on your mind when you wrote your novel? He was the only person to make the connection.)

But to call my novel a conversation with Bowen's book is inaccurate, as the novel was an anticonversation, written in a kind of competition, a kind of antagonism, yet all the time entirely under the spell of *The Death of the Heart*. To articulate it demands honesty that I am almost unwilling to offer. Though evasion rarely leads to joy; there is, one must admit, a sense of joy if one can dissect something, oneself included, with precision. (In college and as a young scientist the tasks I had most enjoyed were the peripheral activities: to peel everything away and leave only the neural system intact in an insect; to harvest the bone marrow from a mouse's femur until the bone became nearly transparent; to carefully flush out a mouse's lungs. Perhaps my deficiency as a scientist, a lack of ultimate purpose, is why I love writing. Precision gives me more pleasure than the end result.)

On a different trip—much later than the London trip—I ran into Portia at the train station on my way to visit Monet's garden at Giverny. Displayed on a bulletin board, advertising an exhibition, was *The Portrait of Marguerite van Mons* by the Belgian painter Théo van Rysselberghe: a black-clad girl, about to open an ornate door, stares out of the painting (or is she closing the door to secure her presence in the room—an entrance rather than an exit?). Thousands of people must have passed through the station that summer, but not many would have recognized Portia—the painting is used as the cover of my paperback edition of *The Death of the Heart*— exiting a drawing room: "Each movement had a touch of exaggeration, as though some secret power kept springing out. At the same time she looked cautious, aware of the world in which she had to live. She was sixteen, losing her childish majesty."

Portia, newly orphaned, is sent to live with her half brother, Thomas, and Anna, Thomas's wife. An orphan is always a melodrama, but Portia is among the most unbearable. Her whole self exposes others' inability to see in life a seriousness that can match hers. She watches the world with an awkward tenacity. Observation, however, is not understanding; neither is it protection. For Portia, every moment is conclusive and catastrophic, and the distinctions between then and now and later are wiped out by her insistence on making every moment as meaningful and definite as life is often not. I feel an annoying kinship with Portia—I bat at such a thought like batting at a fly. To say nothing matters is to admit that everything matters. Like Portia, I too struggle with a lack of depth perception.

Willful, a friend says of Portia; willfully selfish. Indeed, *The Death of the Heart* is a study of selfishness, but great fiction is inevitably a study of selfishness. Some selfishness is more commonplace than others, some more respectable, or more destructive, or more cynical. There is Portia's father, whose timorous selfishness is a contrast to his first wife's castigating selfishness. (He is exiled by his efficient wife into marrying his mistress when she becomes pregnant with Portia.) There is Eddie, who, in his prideful selfishness, destroys Portia's life. (Eddie, a cad with wounded innocence as his core, needs someone to prey on more than a heartless one would.) Thomas and Anna seek convenience in their tidy selfishness, and when they find themselves trapped in Portia's melodrama, even their cold, sensible egos cannot restore their life to being lived on the surface.

Some people, knowing the boundaries of their selves,

choose to disregard what is beyond as inconsequential. Such selfishness may not be honorable, though one has to admire the honesty when Anna admits to reading Portia's diary. "No, it's not at all odd: it's the sort of thing I do do," she says, neither with remorse nor in self-defense.

Portia and Anna, one of Bowen's lovers surmised in his diary, were "the two halves" of Bowen, one with "the naïvety of childhood—or genius," the other "as an outside hostile person might see her." Bowen's genius is that, by setting the two halves against each other, she makes herself invincible.

Bowen's cruelty toward her characters cannot be distinguished from her indulgence. Anna sets her heart to eliminate all emotion. Portia wants nothing but for all people to be softened by feelings—hers about them and theirs about her. If Anna were not so merciless in depriving herself of any real connection, we would lose respect for her. If Portia were not so transparent with love—unsought and unearned—we would be protective of her. Bowen manipulates us to feel most for Anna when she is her coldest self, and exposes us when we take the side of the heartless world to deny Portia the dignity of suffering.

Bowen left no diaries or journals. Perhaps none survived, and one wonders what she would have recorded writing strictly to herself. Or perhaps she was not in the habit of writing something so private and revealing—another reason I feel a kind of antagonism toward her. I feel the necessity of confronting her when I write, as though only by matching what she does can I protect myself from her. What innocence Bowen destroys in her novels I want to destroy with equal resolve. What selfishness Bowen indulges I want to indulge. What violence—psychological more than physical—Bowen makes her characters suffer I want my characters to inflict and endure too. Portia is exposed and betrayed at her most vulnerable moments, and Bowen allows no help from others or herself; it is with the same satisfaction that I have little sympathy for my younger self sitting by a lake with deadly thoughts on a winter day. No, I have sided with the young men riding past her on their bicycles and goading her to jump into the water, with the woman stepping into the courtyard and shooing her away, with the mother who watched the clock and informed her exactly how many minutes late she arrived home, exhausted by indecision.

"I don't know what's going to happen; but I do know what's capable of happening," Seneca wrote in a letter. The terror of that statement is why I write myself into a battle against Bowen—not to converse, which seeks understanding; not to argue, which is intellectual; not to confront, out of artistic disagreement, or misunderstanding, or even jealousy, but to hold on to something essential. "[I am] a writer before I am a woman," she said of herself. Easily I could assert a more absolute position, being a writer before I am a person, or being a writer and nothing more. Bowen makes me aware of what I am capable of becoming; her characters make me aware of what everyone is capable of becoming. This knowledge is what turns me against her yet brings me back to her work. "The moment one is sad one is ordinary," she wrote. But that is not enough. The moment one feels anything one feels fatal.

WHEN LARKIN, AT twenty-eight, compared himself to Eddie or Portia's father, it must have been a statement made from both self-loathing and self-defense. What awareness, what resignation, what passive-aggressiveness led him to write the letter.

"My life is so entirely selfish that mirages of unselfishness tormented me," he wrote to Jones later, again explaining his lack of commitment.

> I long to abandon myself entirely to someone else. The peculiarity of my character is that I never feel that there is *any* mingling—either I don't "abdicate," & the other person loses, or I do, and I lose myself. A monstrous infantile shell of egotism inside which I quietly asphyxiate. To read K.M.'s [Katherine Mansfield's] dreams of a shared life with Murry—this perturbs me greatly. . . . To live quietly and complementarily with another would be extraordinary— almost impossible—I don't know, it's only the fact that I do nothing for anybody that promotes these self-searchings.

The opposite of this extreme charge is that a person does everything for others—an exemplary unselfishness familiar to me all my life. It encapsulates my mother's existence. Before retiring she was a schoolteacher, respected by generations of students and their parents because everything she did, she did for them. My mother is the first person I observed at a close distance, too close perhaps, whose public and private personas have so little in common.

If a person is not living for others, it does not mean he knows how to live for himself. One prefers anyone—a mother, a lover, a friend—who knows how to live for herself. Such knowledge is not selfishness.

Twenty-two years after comparing himself to Portia's Eddie, Larkin was not in any better place.

I'm not so confident about telling the truth as you: not so sure I can, not so sure I want to. I cling to pretence. . . . You *see* this all right, but, I think, interpret it as deliberate and hostile deceit. It doesn't seem like that to me, more like making life livable.

This insufferable effort to make life livable, a refrain throughout Larkin's letters, is the same philosophy that dictates Thomas and Anna's life in *The Death of the Heart*. Even if one finds that frustrating, one has to fear for them. They are sabotaged by Portia, whose every effort is to make life unlivable unless it is lived on her terms.

Larkin's continuous self-accusation and his continuous effort to excuse himself lead me to think he lived an emotionally honest life and bore the pains well. But this impression must have come from reading years of his letters in a few months. Of course he lived through time, endured it even: lone bicycle rides in the rain, unaccompanied evenings of cooking inedible food, long nights of waiting for the broadcast of Handel's music, trouble with friends and family and lovers, quarreling in letters and on the phone with Jones, breakdowns, hurtful silence.

> I'm terrified of the thought of time passing (or whatever is meant by that phrase) whether I "do" anything or not. In a way I may believe, deep down, that doing nothing acts as a brake on "time"—it doesn't of course. It merely adds the torment of having done nothing, when the time comes when it really doesn't matter if you've done anything or not. . . . Perhaps you take more naturally to doing nothing than I do.

I envied Larkin when I read this passage after another hospital stay. My life was on hold. There were diagnoses to grapple with, medications and protocols to implement, hospital staff to report to, but they were there only to eliminate an option. What was to replace it I could not see, but it was not within anyone's capacity to answer.

It is easier to take something away than to give. Giving requires understanding and imagination; taking away requires only resolution and action.

Is the wish to escape suffering selfish? It is considered so with suicide. But even less extreme escapes leave wounds in others' lives. *The Death of the Heart* is not only a study of selfishness, but also a study of the struggle to escape suffering. To whom the damage is done no one wants to ask.

This is the question that unsettles me more: Is suffering selfish?

For as long as I can remember my mother has spoken of me as a selfish person. If I were religious, I would kneel nightly for salvation from this sin. There is no measure to quantify selfishness: how much of oneself is devoted to others, or even which part of life is to be lived and which part given up. All my life I have failed to prove myself unselfish.

Once, when I implored my mother to imagine how my sister must have felt as a child, being made known to be the less pretty, less smart, and thus less favored daughter, my mother started to cry. When she was four, I bought a new blouse for her for the new year even though I didn't feel well enough to go to the store, she said. How can you say I mistreated her? After my children were born, my mother told me several times that she had never tended us at night when we were infants. Your father had to get up and feed you because he knew my sleep should not be disturbed, she said with such genuine pride that I wonder if everything she has done should be looked at again with more understanding. She may be one of the very few indisputably innocent people I have encountered in life.

Can innocence be called selfish? "Innocence always calls mutely for protection when we would be so much wiser to guard ourselves against it: innocence is like a dumb leper who has lost his bell, wandering the world, meaning no harm," Graham Greene writes of Alden Pyle in *The Quiet American*. Only the innocent, I now realize, have the right to denounce selfishness, as the innocent do not have a sense where their selves end and others' start. In fact, their selves do not end. They have one world, complete and consistent. When we enter that world we are intruders; when we exit we are abandoners; when we don't abide by the ruling of innocence, we are betrayers.

(Is Marianne Moore's mother not another figure of innocence? And Turgenev's mother? All mothers are innocent when they accuse their children of selfishness.)

A REAL PERSON, open-ended, can only be approached as a hypothesis. A character in fiction is demanded to be accountable. Some characters are more willing to offer a context. The young women in Jane Austen's novels, for instance, seek happiness and suffer when happiness is made unavailable, by situation, chance, or folly. No character rebels against this demand more than Sue Bridehead in *Jude the Obscure*.

Like Larkin, I'm obsessed with Thomas Hardy, particularly his last novel ("like a street accident," Larkin said of *Jude*). Sue is so incoherent that she raises in my mind the question of believability. Not that I don't believe her as a character—a complaint one sometimes hears as criticism of a less successful character—but I don't believe a character can achieve inexplicability as she has. "Really too irritating not to have been a real person" was Larkin's conclusion, and some biographers have suggested Hardy's first wife as a model.

To say we know a person is to write that person off. This is at times life's necessity. We run out of time or patience or curiosity; or we depart, willingly or not, from the situation that makes investigation possible and necessary. A person written off may become a character—depending on the charity of memory.

When characters forgo realness—their unknowability—they become real and known to a reader. Sue—I worry that this statement will cause confusion or misunderstanding—is too murkily real to be a character. She starts unknowable and ends so, too. Yet despite my frustration with her, she may be the only character in fiction I would go any length to defend.

There is an episode in Sue's life that recalls an episode in Mansfield's life. As a teenager, Mansfield shifted her romantic interest between two brothers. When she was made pregnant by one of them, she hastily married a singer eleven years her senior, but left him the same evening before the marriage was consummated. After a miscarriage and convalescence, she met John Middleton Murry. The two began a relationship, then broke up twice before her previous marriage was legally dissolved and they married.

Sue, a generation before Mansfield, is living with a university student in a platonic relationship before she meets Jude. Her attitude toward Jude, "all this no-you-mustn't-love-me-well-perhaps-if-you-like-you-may stuff" as Larkin impatiently put it, is read by many, including V. S. Pritchett and Larkin, as coquetry. Still, I find her actions more elusive: her hasty choice to enter a marriage with an older man despite her distaste for him and sex in general; her childish insistence that Jude walk down the church aisle with her, like a married couple, right before her wedding; her impulsive decision to leave her husband for Jude on the condition that they maintain a relationship without any physical contact (and later leaving Jude to remarry her first husband); her acquiescence, eventually, to becoming Jude's lover while refusing to accept marriage. This "colossal inconstancy," one suspects, is what Hardy intends as the essence of her character. "Sue's logic was extraordinarily compounded, and seemed to maintain that before a thing was done it might be right to do, but that being done it became wrong; or, in other words, that things which were right in theory were wrong in practice."

A good drama could be made of a bohemian Mansfield. She is one of those who tirelessly create contexts for themselves. Nothing—her misjudgments, her unpredictability, the suffering she caused others and herself—would affect our understanding and perhaps even love of her as a character. There are telling details from her journals—passing thoughts, gnawing pains, brilliant sentences that would later find places in her stories. My favorites are the expense lists: mostly entries for daily food, but unfailingly there are envelopes, letter paper, stamps, and sometimes telegrams, altogether more costly than food. Other small expenses I like to read about, too—curtains, boot polish, hair pin, "bill with sewing woman," "safety pin for Jack," and "laundry(!)." (In the diaries of Virginia Woolf—her friend and rival—one reads about teas and lunches, rarely the expenses.)

Sue remains incomprehensible. "I wonder what he was doing exactly," Larkin puzzled over Hardy's design for her. He could have made her a credible character who fascinates and frustrates with her indecision and ambivalence. He treats other characters—even the least sympathetic—with the more thoughtful touch of a novelist.

For instance, Arabella, Jude's first wife. If Hardy intends for readers to feel repelled by her vulgarity, dishonesty, and coldness, he also grants her unmistakable vitality. There is no ambivalence but her strong desire to make something out of a life that doesn't offer much. We see Arabella as a young woman, practicing sucking in her cheeks to make dimples. Later in the novel, during an encounter with Sue, Arabella, lying with her back to the door and thinking that the person entering the room is Jude, takes her time to remake her seducing dimples, only to recognize the futility when Sue speaks.

The preface to the first edition ends with this preemptive statement: "*Jude the Obscure* is simply an endeavour to give shape and coherence to a series of seemings, or personal impressions, the questions of their consistency or their discordance, of their permanence or their transitoriness, being regarded as not of the first moment." The seemings really only come with Sue. What makes Hardy deprive her of the shape and coherence that he grants other characters?

At the end of the novel, by Jude's graveside, Arabella speaks about Sue with vengeful truth: "She's never found peace since she left his arms, and never will till she is as he is now!" A writer's cruelty is to exile a real person to fiction. She is forced to give up her unknowability. When she defies that fate she is defenseless against the readers, who deem her an unsuccessful character.

But when I question Hardy's unfairness, am I not making the common mistake of conflating a character with the writer or someone in his life? One can examine a writer's work and biography with a detective's eye for convincing and alluring details. Ernest Hemingway's defense of his infidelity in a letter to his father: "You are fortunate enough to have only been in love with one woman in your life"; Virginia Woolf's jealousy of Mansfield during the latter's life and after her death in her diary: "Do people always get what they deserve, & did K.M. do something to deserve this cheap posthumous life? & am I jealous even now?" It is no surprise we continue to see writers become characters: Hemingway, Woolf, and even Larkin, with his love life dramatized for the screen. Stripped of realness, their fame and idiosyncrasy, their expeditions internal and external all heighten their characterness and make engaging stories. A reader's cruelty is to return writers to characters. And reading their journals and letters is the reliable first step.

In a letter Larkin contemplated Tryphena Sparks, Hardy's cousin, proposed by some as the real model for Sue. (There was the conjecture that Tryphena was an early lover of Hardy's; perhaps there was a child born, too.) "But it would be disappointing to me if it were true—first, because I've always thought TH a non bastard, & secondly I should hate him to have some *reason* for being gloomy—I thought he & he alone saw the inherent misery of life."

Why does Sue Bridehead *matter* so much? I wished I could have this conversation with Larkin. I wished I could ask Hardy this question, too. I reread other Hardy novels, and the letters of Hardy's two wives. I spent my days reading novels whose characters crossed paths only in my mind; I was reading writers' diaries and biographies connected by footnotes. I did not see people outside the

132 / Yiyun Li

household often; I did not talk with anyone but one friend by phone. Isolation, I was reminded again and again, is a danger. But what if one's real context is in books? Some days, going from one book to another, preoccupied with thoughts that were of no importance, I would feel a rare moment of serenity: all that could not be solved in my life was merely a trifle as long as I kept it at a distance. Between that suspended life and myself were these dead people and imagined characters. One could spend one's days among them as a child arranges a circle of stuffed animals when the darkness of night closes in.

I ALMOST LOST Larkin's letters once. My bag was stolen, and for half a day I was distraught. After paying a ransom, I reunited with Larkin's letters, a thick volume by Kierkegaard, and my journal. A computer, a wallet, and a handful of pens became other people's possessions.

A violation of privacy, someone said about my stolen journal, sympathizing. Yet that was not my concern. The thief, to whom my journal was a material opportunity, could not invade my privacy—the arguments recorded in it would only be repetitions of a cuckoo clock to an outsider. But this interruption exposed the illusion in which my life was lived. To lose the journal was to lose continuity from one day to the next. To lose the books—*my* copies—was to lose the conversations. And conversations are my evidence of time. I seal up journals and shelve books, but they still are my permanency. Unlike human lives and feelings, they are not written in vanishing ink.

MANSFIELD IS ONE of the most frequently mentioned authors in Larkin's letters. In analyzing her life and love affairs, Larkin is talking about himself. Reading them at the same time, I was constantly offering my own interpretation, defending Mansfield or disagreeing with Larkin's defense of her. More acutely, I was aware that my obsession with them reflected what I resent in myself: seclusion, self-deception, and above all the need—the neediness—to find shelter from one's uncertain self in other lives. For Mansfield, it was Chekhov; for Larkin, it was Mansfield and Hardy. It is characteristic of both that Mansfield chose someone she aspired to be, and Larkin, those who would condone his weaknesses.

When Larkin sent Jones an advance copy of *The Whitsun Weddings,* without warning her that it included a love poem to another woman, Jones was incredulous. Larkin replied in his typical dodging, thus telling, manner:

> My excuse—or if it isn't an excuse, my answer—is, as you might expect, a complete forgetfulness: I didn't hesitate a moment about including it, because I didn't think it wd bother you, and it seemed good enough. . . . I'm sorry about *Broadcast,* and I'm sure

my distress was real. I suppose I don't really equate poems with real-life as most people do—I mean they are true in a way, but very much dolled up & censored.

I do not equate writing with real life either—if cornered I would agree with Larkin, but I am unable to articulate what real life is. "If no one ever read me, would I write? Perhaps not; but I would not be able to stop writing in my head," V. S. Pritchett said in a letter to Elizabeth Bowen. Of course writing is essential for a writer, and being read, too—halfheartedly I repeat his conviction to others and myself. But the truth is I did not connect those necessities to a writer's life until I read Pritchett's letter. Writing is an option, so is not writing; being read is a possibility, so is not being read. Reading, however, I equate with real life: life can be opened and closed like a book; living is a choice, so is not living.

Saying these words aloud puts me in fear that I am again getting things wrong—not that others will disagree or misread me, but that the nearer I get to what I want to say, the further I deviate from it. Any word is the wrong word when it is too close to the unspeakable.

I am aware that, every time I have a conversation with a book, I benefit from someone's decision against silence. Still, I am greedy for what I am deprived: I have a friend who erases many sentences before putting down one; another friend keeps her thoughts to herself. Yet I believe that there is a truth that is truer in the unexpressed; having spoken, I am apprehensive that I no longer have a claim to that truth.

Why then write to trap oneself? Innocence—the kind Bowen describes in *The Death of the Heart*—is the answer I can provide:

> Innocence so constantly finds itself in a false position that inwardly innocent people learn to be disingenuous. Finding no language in which to speak in their own terms, they resign themselves to being translated imperfectly. They exist alone; when they try to enter into relations they compromise falsifyingly— through anxiety, through desire to impart and to feel warmth. The system of our affections is too corrupt for them. They are bound to blunder, then to be told they cheat. In love, the sweetness and violence they have to offer involves a thousand betrayals for the less innocent. Incurable strangers to the world, they never cease to exact a heroic happiness. Their singleness, their ruthlessness, their one continuous wish makes them bound to be cruel, and to suffer cruelty.

It seems wise, in life, to shun the innocent. But in truth innocence grows on one. I have been thinking about Sue and Portia. I have been thinking about my mother, too. It is easier to live among characters—others' and my own. Even those real people whose lives passed become characters in reading. They would never detect my innocence. And it is out of innocence that I write.

I left London without a decision about the novel. When I returned home I looked up an earlier letter from Trevor, with a query about another novel. *How is the novel? One asks that as one does about an ill person, and a novel that's not yet finished is rather like that. You reach the end and the thing is either dead or in much better shape. The dead should be left in peace.*

To Speak Is to Blunder
but I Venture

In a dream the other night I was back in Beijing, at the entrance of our apartment complex, where a public telephone, a black rotary, had once been guarded by the old women from the neighborhood association. They used to listen without hiding their disdain or curiosity while I was on the phone with friends; when I finished, they would complain about the length of the conversation before logging it into their book and calculating the charge. In those days I gathered many chores before I went to use the telephone lest my parents noticed my extended absence. My allowance—which was what I could scrimp and save from my lunch money—was spent on phone calls and stamps and envelopes. Like a Victorian character I checked our mail before my parents did and intercepted letters meant for me. To think that eager person—not wanting to miss a connection with the world—would grow up into the recluse I prefer to think of myself as today: there must be a part of everyone's youth that later one avoids looking at too closely.

In my dream I asked for the phone. Two women came out of the office. I recognized them. In real life they are both gone. No, they said; the service is no longer offered because everyone has a cellphone these days. There was nothing remarkable about the dream—a melancholy visit to the past is beyond one's control—but for the fact that the women spoke to me in English.

When I started writing, my husband asked if I understood the implication of my decision. What he meant were not the practical concerns, though there were plenty: the nebulous hope of getting published, the lack of a career certainty as had been laid out in science, the harsher immigration regulations. Many of my college classmates, as scientists, acquired their green cards under the category of national interest waiver. An artist is not of much importance to any nation's interest.

My husband's question was about language. Did I understand what it meant to renounce my mother tongue?

Nabokov once answered a question he must have been tired of being asked: "My private tragedy, which cannot, indeed should not, be anybody's concern, is that I had to abandon my natural language." That something is called a tragedy, however, means it is no longer personal. One weeps out of private pain, but only when the audience swarms in to claim understanding and empathy do they call it tragedy. One's grief belongs to oneself; one's tragedy, to others.

I feel a tinge of guilt when I imagine Nabokov's woe. Like all intimacies, the intimacy between one and one's mother tongue can demand more than one is willing to give, or what one is capable of giving. If I allow myself to be honest, I would borrow from Nabokov for a stronger and stranger statement. My private salvation, which cannot and should not be anybody's concern, is that I disowned my native language.

For a while, when I was unwell, my dreams often went back to Beijing, standing on top of a building—one of those gray, Soviet-styled apartment buildings—or being lost on a bus running through an unfamiliar neighborhood. Waking up from these dreams, I would list in my journal memories that did not appear in my dream: a swallow nest underneath a balcony, the barbed wire on the rooftop, the garden where old people sat and exchanged gossip, the post bins at street corners, round, green, covered by dust, with handwritten collection times behind a square window of half-opaque plastic.

Yet I have never dreamed about Iowa City, where I first landed in America. When asked about my initial impression of the place, I cannot excavate anything from memory to form a meaningful answer. During a recent trip there I visited the neighborhood I used to walk past every day. The one-story houses, which were painted in pleasantly muted colors, with gardens in the front enclosed by white picket fences, had not changed. I realized that I had never described them to others or to myself in Chinese, and by the time English was established as my language they had become everyday mundanities. What happened during my transition from one language to another did not become memory.

To OWN—A HOUSE, a life on a quiet street, a language, a dream—is to allow oneself to be owned, too. The moment the present slips into the past owning starts to be replaced by disowning. Why wait for the inevitable?

People often ask about my decision to write in English. The switch from one language to another feels natural to me, I reply, though that does not say much, just as one can hardly give a convincing explanation why someone's hair turns gray on this day but not on the other, or why some birds fly south when the temperature drops. But these are inane analogies, used as excuses because I do not want to touch the heart of the matter. Yes, there is something unnatural, which I have refused to accept. Not that I write in a second language—there are always Nabokov and Conrad as references, and many of my contemporaries as well; nor that I impulsively gave up a reliable career for writing. It's the absoluteness of the abandonment—with such determination that it is a kind of suicide.

The tragedy of Nabokov's loss is that his misfortune was easily explained by public history—his story became other people's possession. My decision to write in English has also been explained as a flight from my country's history. But unlike Nabokov, who had been a Russian writer, I never wrote in Chinese. Still, one has little control over how one's work is received, and one cannot avoid having a private decision, once seen through a public prism, become a metaphor. Once a poet of Eastern European origin and I—we both have lived in America for years, and both write in English—were asked to read our work in our native languages at a gala. But I don't write in Chinese, I explained, and the organizer apologized for her misunderstanding. I offered to read Li Po or Du Fu or any of the ancient poets I grew up memorizing, but instead it was arranged for me to read the poems of a political prisoner.

A metaphor's desire to transcend diminishes any human story; its ambition to illuminate blinds those who create metaphors. In my distrust of metaphors I feel a kinship to George Eliot: "We all of us, grave or light, get our thoughts entangled in metaphors, and act fatally on the strength of them." This, I know, is what my husband was questioning years ago. But my abandonment of my first language is personal, so deeply personal that I resist any interpretation—political or historical or ethnographical.

. . .

CHINESE IMMIGRANTS OF my generation in America criticize my English for not being native enough. A compatriot emailed, pointing out how my language is neither lavish nor lyrical, as a real writer's language should be; you only write simple things in simple English, you should be ashamed of yourself, he wrote in a fury. A professor in graduate school told me I should stop writing, as English would remain a foreign language to me. Their concerns about ownership of a language, rather than making me impatient like Nabokov, allow me secret laughter. English is to me as random a choice as any other language. What one goes toward is less definitive than that from which one turns away.

Before I left China I destroyed the journals I had kept for years and most of the letters written to me (what I could not bring myself to destroy I sealed up and have never opened); my letters to others I would have destroyed too, had I had them. But one's relationship with a native language is similar to that with the past. There is not a moment one could point to and say: this is the beginning of my past, or this is the beginning of my relationship with my mother tongue, up until that moment I was free. What comes before—other people's past, other people's relationship with that language—claims a right against one's will. Rarely does a story start where we wish it had, or end where we wish it would.

. . .

ONE CROSSES THE border to become a new person. One finishes a manuscript and cuts off the characters. One adopts a language. These are false and forced frameworks, providing illusory freedom, as time provides illusory leniency when we, in anguish, let it pass monotonously. *To kill time*—an English phrase that still chills me: time can be killed but only by frivolous matters and purposeless activities. No one thinks of suicide as a courageous endeavor to kill time.

In the hospital, a group of nursing students came to play bingo one Friday night. A young woman asked if I would join her. Bingo, I said; I've never in my life played. She thought for a moment and said that she had only played bingo in the hospital. It was her eighth hospitalization; she had been schooled for a while in the hospital, and once she pointed out a small patch of fenced-in green where she and other children had been let out to exercise. Often her father visited her in the afternoon, and I would watch them sitting together playing a game, not attempting conversation. By then, all words must have been inadequate; language does little to help a mind survive time.

Yet language is capable of sinking a mind. One's thoughts are slavishly bound to language. I used to think an abyss is a moment of despair becoming interminable, but any moment, even the direst, is bound to end. What is abysmal is that one's erratic language closes on one as quicksand. Yet what is spoken by others—truth as cliché, cliché as the only truth—is as indisputable as the retreating solid ground, getting further and further beyond reach. The abyss is that time is annulled by language. We can kill time, but language kills us.

"Patient stated that she felt like a burden to loved ones"—much later, when I read the notes from the emergency room, I did not have any recollection of the conversation. *A burden to loved ones*: this language must have been provided to me. I would never use the phrase in my thinking or writing. But my resistance has little to do with avoiding a platitude. To say a burden is to grant oneself weight in other people's lives; to call them loved ones is to fake one's ability to love. One does not always want to subject oneself to self-interrogation imposed by a cliché.

WHEN KATHERINE MANSFIELD was still a teenager in New Zealand, she wrote in her journal about a man next door playing for weeks on a cornet "Swanee River." "I wake up with the 'Swanee River,' eat it with every meal I take, and go to bed eventually with 'all de world am sad and weary' as a lullaby." I read Mansfield's notebooks and Marianne Moore's letters around the same time. Moore in a letter described a fundraiser at Bryn Mawr, maidens in bathing suits and green bathing tails on a raft: "It was really most realistic . . . way down upon the Swanee river."

I marked the entries because they reminded me of a moment I had forgotten. I was nine, and my sister thirteen. On a Saturday afternoon, I was in our apartment and she was on the balcony. My sister joined the middle-school choir that year, and in the autumn sunshine she sang in a voice that was beginning to leave girlhood. *Way down upon the Swanee River. Far, far away. That's where my heart is turning ever; That's where the old folks stay.*

The lyrics were in Chinese. The memory too should be in Chinese. But I cannot see our tiny garden with the grapevine, which our father cultivated and which later was uprooted by our wrathful mother, or the bamboo fence dotted with morning glories, or the junk that occupied half the balcony, years of accumulations piled high by our father, if I do not name these things to myself in English. I cannot see my sister, but I can hear her sing the lyrics in English.

Over the years my brain has banished Chinese. I dream in English. I talk to myself in English. And memories—not only those about America but also those about China; not only those carried on but also those archived with the wish to forget—are sorted in English. To be orphaned from my native language felt, and still feels, a crucial decision.

Would you ever consider writing in Chinese? an editor from China asked, as many had asked before. I said I doubted it. But don't you want to be part of contemporary Chinese literature? he asked. I have declined to have my books translated into Chinese, which is understood by some as odiously pretentious. Once in a while my mother will comment, hinting at my selfishness, that I have deprived her of the pleasure of reading my books. But Chinese was never my private language. And it will never be.

That I write in English—does it make me part of something else? The verdict of my professor in graduate school was that I was writing in a language that did not belong to me, hence I would not, and should not, belong. But his protest was irrelevant. I have not been using the language to be part of something.

WHEN WE ENTER a world—a new country, a new school, a party, a family or a class reunion, an army camp, a hospital—we speak the language it requires. The wisdom to adapt is the wisdom to have two languages: the one spoken by others, and the one spoken to oneself. One learns to master the public language not much differently from the way one acquires a second language: assess the situations, construct sentences with the right words and the correct syntax, catch a mistake if one can avoid it, or else apologize and learn the lesson after a blunder. Fluency in the public language, like fluency in a second language, can be achieved with enough practice.

Perhaps the line between the two languages—the public and the private—is, and should be, fluid; it is never so for me. I often forget, when I write, that English is also used by others. English is my private language. Every word has to be pondered over before it becomes my word. I have no doubt—can this be an illusion?—that the conversation I have with myself, however linguistically flawed, is the conversation that I have always wanted, in the exact way I want it to be.

In my relationship with English, in this relationship with its intrinsic distance that makes people look askance, I feel invisible but not estranged. It is the position I believe I always want in life. But with every pursuit there is the danger of crossing a line, from invisibility to erasure.

There was a time I could write well in Chinese. In school my essays were used as models; in the army, our squad leader gave me the choice between drafting a speech for her and cleaning the toilets or the pigsties—I always chose to write. Once in high school, several classmates and I entered an oratory contest. The winner would represent the class in a patriotic event. When I went onstage, for some mischievous reason, I saw to it that many of the listeners were moved to tears by the poetic and insincere lies I had made up; I moved myself to tears, too. That I could become a successful propaganda writer crossed my mind. I was disturbed. A young person wants to be true to herself and to the world. But what did not occur to me then was to ask: Can one's intelligence rely entirely on the public language; can one form a precise thought, recall an accurate memory, or even feel a genuine feeling, with only the public language?

My mother, who loves to sing, often sings the songs from her childhood and youth, many of them propaganda from the 1950s and 1960s, but there is one song she has reminisced about all her life because she does not know how to sing it. She learned the song in kindergarten, the year Communism took over her hometown; she can only remember the opening line.

There was an old woman in the hospital who sat in the hallway with a pair of shiny red shoes. I feel like Dorothy, she said as she showed me the shoes, which she had chosen from the donations to patients. Some days her mind was lucid, and she would talk about the red shoes that hurt her feet or the medication that made her brain feel dead and left her body in pain. Other days she talked to the air, an endless conversation with the unseen. People who had abandoned her by going away or dying returned and made her weep.

I often sat next to this lonesome Dorothy. Was I eavesdropping? Perhaps, but her conversation was beyond encroachment. That one could reach a point where the border between public and private language no longer matters is frightening. Much of what one does—to avoid suffering, to seek happiness, to stay healthy—is to keep a safe space for one's private language. The automatic participation in life, however, can turn that space into a secured tomb. Those who have lost that space have only one language left. My grandmother, according to my mother and her siblings, had become a woman who talked to the unseen before being sent to the asylum to die. There is so much to give up: hope, freedom, dignity.

A private language defies any confinement. Death alone can take it away.

MANSFIELD SPOKE OF her habit of keeping a journal as "being garrulous . . . I must say nothing affords me the same relief." Reading her journals presents a dilemma. Several times she directly addressed the readers—her posterity—in a taunting manner. I would prefer to distrust her. But it would be dishonest not to acknowledge the solace of reading them. Not having the exact language for the bleakness I felt, I devoured her words like thirst-quenching poison. Is it possible that one can be held hostage by someone else's words? What I underlined and reread: Are they her thoughts or mine?

> There is nought to do but WORK, but how can I work when this awful weakness makes even the pen like a walking stick.

> There is something profound & terrible in this eternal desire to establish contact.

> It is astonishing how violently a big branch shakes when a silly little bird has left it. I expect the bird knows it and feels immensely arrogant.

> One only wants to feel sure of another. That's all.

I realise my faults better than anyone else could realise them. I know exactly where I fail.

Have people, apart from those far away people, ever existed for me? Or have they always failed me, and faded because I denied them reality? Supposing I were to die, as I sit at this table, playing with my indian paper knife—what would be the difference. No difference at all. Then why don't I commit suicide?

WHEN ONE THINKS in an adopted language, one arranges and rearranges words that are neutral, indifferent even, to arrive at a thought that one does not know to be there.

When one remembers in an adopted language, there is a dividing line in that remembrance. What came before could be someone else's life; it might as well be fiction. Sometimes I think it is this distancing that marks me as coldhearted and selfish. To forget the past is a betrayal, we were taught in school when young; to disown memories is a sin.

What language does one use to feel; or, does one need a language to feel? In the hospital, I visited a class of medical students studying minds and brains. After an interview, the doctor who led the class asked about feelings. I said it was beyond my ability to describe what might as well be indescribable.

If you can be articulate about your thoughts, why can't you articulate your feelings? asked the doctor.

It took me a year to figure out the answer. It is hard to feel in an adopted language, yet it is impossible to do that in my native language.

OFTEN I THINK that writing is a futile effort; so is reading; so is living. Loneliness is the inability to speak with another in one's private language. That emptiness is filled with public language or romanticized connections. But one must be cautious when assuming meaning. A moment of recognition between two people only highlights the inadequacy of language. What can be spoken does not sustain; what cannot be spoken undermines.

After the dream of the public telephone, I remembered a moment in the army. It was New Year's Eve, and we were ordered to watch the official celebration on CCTV. Halfway through the program, a girl on duty came and said there was a long-distance call for me.

It was the same type of black rotary we had back at the apartment complex, and my sister was on the phone. It was the first long-distance call I had received in my life. The next time would be four years later, when an American professor phoned to interview me. I still remember the woman, calling from Mount Sinai Hospital in New York City, asking questions about my interests in immunology, talking about her research projects and life in

America. My English was good enough for me to understand half of what she said, and the scratching noises in the background made me sweat for the missed half.

Yet what did my sister and I talk about on that New Year's Eve? In abandoning my native language I have erased myself from that memory. I have often been asked if—or else told that—English allows me the freedom of expression. As if in taking up another language one can become someone new. But erasing does not stop with a new language, and that, my friend, is my sorrow and my selfishness. In speaking and in writing in an adopted language I have not stopped erasing. I have crossed the line, too, from erasing myself to erasing others. I am not the only casualty in this war against myself.

In an ideal world I would prefer to have my mind reserved for thinking, and thinking alone. I dread the moment when a thought trails off and a feeling starts, when one faces the eternal challenge of eluding the void for which one does not have words. To speak when one cannot is to blunder. I have spoken by having written—this book or any book; for myself and against myself. The solace is with the language I chose. The grief, to have spoken at all.

Either/Or: A Chorus
of Miscellany

Everything a writer produces is posthumous.
—Kierkegaard, *Either/Or*

Once someone followed me across a parking lot after a reading, insisting that I should be not a writer but a stand-up comedian. Once an interviewer told me I was "well mannered" considering how dark some of my characters were. Once someone mentioned to a friend that she had thought I was "a little polite immigrant" and was surprised when I turned out to be "feisty" at an event she attended. Too often people ask why I write about melancholy and loneliness and despondency while I appear to be such a happy person.

Happiness and bleakness are not Orion and Scorpius, unable to occupy the same space in one's emotional sky. Darkness has little to do with good manners; feistiness is irrelevant to politeness. I never set out to write about melancholy and loneliness and despondency. I keep my self to myself and I do not impose on my characters' fates; among them I am as private as I am in life. The posthumous reputation of one's words, truthful or misleading, is a eulogy given by others.

Who is this reader we talk about and start to resent before we even meet him?
—a student from the Iowa Writers' Workshop

A writer and a reader should never be allowed to meet. They live in different time frames. When a book takes on a life for a reader it is already dead for the writer.

It is preposterous for the writer or the reader to trespass, yet both sides often dismiss the border set by the characters: when a writer insists on his presence (on the page, between the lines) to dictate how his work is to be read; or when a reader reads without true curiosity about the characters, but with a goal of judging the writer.

I have read your article very attentively. It is rather difficult for an author to judge fairly a critical analysis of his own works—I must confess that I, for instance, find always the praise too great and the blame too weak. I do not attribute this impression to diffidence or modesty: it is perhaps one of the many disguises which self-love enjoys in.
—Turgenev to Henry James, on the latter's review of Turgenev's work

Diderot has said somewhere: "Avant sa mort l'homme
suit plusieurs fois son propre convoi." ["A man fol-
lows his own funeral procession several times before
he dies."] And now I have had to walk behind my
own literary coffin.

—Turgenev to his brother, on his
contemporaries' attacks on *Virgin Soil*

A successful writer, who lives in isolation, told me that for a decade he had written privately and entertained the idea of accumulating his life's work in a drawer. At his death people would discover his genius, he imagined, but he would not be around to be responsible for his words.

Perhaps only an absolute kind of self-love justifies such a belief. Most of us don't seek this extremity. Without life there would not be death. Is it bravery or cowardice that a writer consoles himself with this thought when he parades after his literary coffin?

Author of Chinese Origin Wins Big Prize in UK; Ac-
cused of Selling China to Court Biased Westerners

—news report, April 2015

It was the first real spring day after a long Midwestern winter. I was browsing news websites, both in English and in Chinese, in a sunny hotel lounge in Chicago. Returning to that city was like returning to one's youth.

When I first arrived in America, I had traveled there for an immunology conference. It was the week before Thanksgiving, and I stood on Michigan Avenue, watching Americans watching the parade, amazed that they would volunteer to attend such a festivity with unconcealed happiness. I had been to celebrations and parades in Tiananmen Square, too, though they had all been political assignments. Still, some memories bring a sense of loss for Beijing. The giant portraits—two stories high—along Chang'an Boulevard: Marx, Engels, Lenin, and Stalin, the first four foreigners' names and faces every child in my generation had learned by heart. Nostalgia does not always align with politics.

I was thinking about noting that feeling in my journal when I clicked the link to the article about the Chinese writer, and was confronted by my own name and face.

The inevitability of a full circle: one writes to escape the omniscient voice that defines one, only to come to the same omniscient voice that takes the liberty to define one's work as well as one's self.

Perhaps the greatest pressure on the writer comes from the society within society: his political or religious group, even it may be his university or his employers. It does seem to me that one privilege he can claim, in common perhaps with his fellow human beings, but possibly with greater safety, is that of disloy-

alty. . . . Disloyalty is our privilege. But it is a
privilege you will never get society to recognize. All
the more necessary that we who can be disloyal with
impunity should keep that ideal alive.

—Graham Greene to Elizabeth Bowen

I am used to being seen by some Chinese—both in the West and in China—as a cultural traitor. Why can't she write in Chinese? people ask; if she doesn't write in Chinese, what right does she have to write about our country?

The collective feelings of a group are oftentimes more fragile than an individual's feelings. I feel little remorse when a group of people, out of hurt feelings, accuse me of any sin. Writing, as long as it is one's private freedom, will always be disloyalty.

The individual does not fight external enemies; it is
with itself and its love that it fights it out, of its own
accord.

—Kierkegaard, *Either/Or*

Before I left Chicago my mother called and quoted the negativity in China, which had been reported to her by my sister. The thought then occurred to me that the news must have been seen by my husband, too, who visits the same Chinese news websites as I do. To know that my family would witness my name being abused: What are my obligations to them?

Writing is a confusing business. One's inner clock, set to an exclusively private time, is bound only to what one writes. Life is lived in a different time zone. Caught in between is one's family. To protect them from the internal clock, one risks alienating them; to include them, one risks intrusion.

> *I have so many stories to tell you. I think you should write a book about them yet you have no interest in them.*
>
> —My mother on the phone

> *I don't think that's what she wants.*
>
> —My father on the phone

Years ago, when I was defending a collection of essays as a thesis, a writer on the committee asked about my mother's absence from the narrative. A mother is not always central to a story, I said; perhaps my mother is only a flat character. If that's the case, he said, we would appreciate learning it. That she is a flat character? I said. No, that you think she is, he corrected me.

Not writing, like writing, can be disloyalty, too. If one turns away from the storytelling of one's mother, is it worse than turning away from one's motherland and mother tongue?

What's interesting to me is writers' drive to express themselves. Not all people have such desire.

> —My husband

Is it really to express myself that I write? Not if I think about what it is in myself that needs to be expressed: hardly anything new. This tireless drive to write must have something to do with what cannot be told.

Stories I find difficult to tell: a year into college my mother quit school and moved to Beijing to be near her mother, who was to die within a year. Having broken the residency and education ruling, my mother did not receive a food ration, and my grandmother would starve herself until the end of her life for my mother.

Stories I refuse to tell: my mother's either/or. Do you want a mad mother, she asked us all the time, or a dead mother? The assumption that no one wants a dead mother condones all behavior.

Stories I want to forget: my husband said that every phone call I made from the hospital started with a query about my mother. You have your children, he said, and she is not among them.

Something wonderful happened to me. I was transported into the seventh heaven. All the gods sat there in assembly. By special grace I was accorded the favour of a wish. "Will you," said Mercury, "have youth, or beauty, or power, or a long life, or the pret-

> tiest girl, or any other of the many splendours we have
> in our chest of knick-knacks? So choose, but just one
> thing." For a moment I was at a loss. Then I ad-
> dressed myself to the gods as follows: "Esteemed con-
> temporaries, I choose one thing: always to have the
> laughter on my side." Not a single word did one god
> offer in answer; on the contrary they all began to
> laugh. From this I concluded that my prayer was ful-
> filled and that the gods knew how to express them-
> selves with taste, for it would hardly have been fitting
> gravely to answer, "It has been granted you."
>
> —Kierkegaard, *Either/Or*

The same day my mother reported the news from China, a high-school classmate, whom I had not had contact with for over twenty years, sent me an email and attached anonymous comments exchanged by our classmates. Having not been in touch with any of them for years, I was taken aback by the malevolence of the messages: jeering at a present person they don't know, mixed with mocking the teenager I was. The man who sent me the email had once asked me to kiss him. Why? I had asked, being eighteen and having not the remotest inclination to do so. I forget what reason he gave me or how I declined, but the past, having passed, always comes back to claim what it has no right to. Worse than people who refuse to come into one's stories are those who insist on taking a place.

*Compared with the internal, the external becomes in-
significant and of no consequence. The point in reflec-
tive sorrow is that the sorrow is constantly in search
of its object; the searching is the unrest of sorrow and
its life.*

—Kierkegaard, *Either/Or*

The one time during this difficult period I truly laughed
without any restraint, it was one of those days when I sat
on a ward couch and saw little hope in life. Another patient grabbed *War and Peace* from my hands, and, with
R-rated language, scolded me for messing up my brain
with nonsense. Her grievance against Tolstoy was so personal that I could not stop laughing.

Have I made you laugh? she said. She then raised the
thick volume. Has this fucking book ever made you
laugh? No! It's so damn heavy it could kill me.

Well, what do you want me to do, I said; I can't change
myself.

Laugh more, she said.

Laughter needs a target, I wanted to say; it is not an
argument but a judgment; I would rather argue than
judge. These thoughts, circling in my head, made me
laugh at myself.

When people insist that I look too happy for my work,
or my work is too bleak for my appearance, I resort to
glibness. Oh, I say, there is that wonderfully woeful Kier-

kegaard. For a year, when I could not save myself from despair, I read him obsessively. He has made me laugh more than any other writer.

> *A long story has after all a measureable length; on the other hand, a short story sometimes has the puzzling property of being longer than the most long-drawn-out one.*
>
> —Kierkegaard, *Either/Or*

One summer, my twelve-year-old read *Les Misérables* three times, cover to cover. I tried in vain to convince him that it is not the only great novel, and Victor Hugo not the only great writer (not even the only great French writer, I said to him).

A young person, beginning to read seriously, tends to live—infatuated, even—with one book at a time. The world offered by the book is large enough to contain all other worlds, or exclusive enough to make all other worlds retreat. Sometimes the book is replaced by another, the old world giving way to a new one; the enchantment—or the entrapment—may also be an experience that happens once in life.

> *Solitude is noble, but fatal to an artist who has not the strength to break out of it. An artist must live the life of his own time, even if it be clamorous and impure:*

he must forever be giving and receiving, and giving,
and giving, and again receiving.

—Romain Rolland, *Jean-Christophe*

A few years ago, I discovered in a secondhand bookstore a copy of the English translation of *Jean-Christophe*. The novel was originally published in 1910. In the 1938 Modern Library edition, which was what I found, the author's name is followed only by the birth year: Romain Rolland (1866–). The owner of the book had his name, an Edward G———, and the date "October 30, 1943" written inside the cover. Rolland was still alive when the book was purchased: its owner was a contemporary. Other than that mark, he did not underline the text or comment in the margin.

Between ages sixteen and eighteen, I read the Chinese translation of *Jean-Christophe* many times. When I first arrived in America, with a French grammar book and a dictionary and without any previous knowledge of the language, I set out to read the original French text along with its English translation, both from the university library, where they had sat for decades without having been checked out. I thought it would be a good way to improve my English and to learn French with a novel that I had half memorized. I did not reach Volume Two before both editions were due.

Rolland, novelist, playwright, music critic, biographer, and Nobel laureate, has long been forgotten in this country, partly, I suppose, for the reason that he was a Communist (on top of being a Frenchman!).

When one is younger, one tends to read without a context—or what is considered as context is only a pretext. A love story is preparation for love, a sad tale paves the road to sadness, an epic an experience of honor and glory. It is the same with living. One learns to understand and make peace with one's context, rather than going from one pretext to the next. The latter is an experience with which I have been familiar. For years I have had the belief that all my questions will be answered by the books I am reading. Books, however, only lead to other books.

It is surprising now to think that *Jean-Christophe*, a novel about being political, about participating in life, was at one time the novel that offered me the entire world. Would I even believe in Rolland's words today? I have finally come to the point where I know the answers I look for are not in any book.

I said how my own character seemed to cut out a shape like a shadow in front of me. This she understood (I give it as an example of her understanding) & proved it by telling me that she thought this bad: one ought to merge into things.

—Virginia Woolf in her diary, on her
last meeting with Katherine Mansfield

Virginia Woolf and Katherine Mansfield had an intense and uneasy friendship, as is often found between two rivals who also understand each other.

A shadowy shape cut out and placed in front of one's own eyes is not a character, but a phantom. *To merge into things*—there is a Chekhovian echo in Mansfield's phrase. After Mansfield's death, Woolf criticized that Mansfield could not "put thoughts, or feelings, or subtleties of any kind into her characters, without at once becoming, where she is serious, hard, and where she is sympathetic, sentimental."

She [Katherine Mansfield] said a good deal about feeling things deeply: also about being pure, which I wont criticise, though of course I very well could. But now what do I feel about my *writing?—this book, that is,* The Hours, *if thats its name? One must write from deep feeling, said Dostoevsky. And do I? Or do I fabricate with words, loving them as I do? No I think not. In this book I have almost too many ideas. I want to give life & death, sanity & insanity; I want to criticise the social system, & to show it at work, at its most intense— But here I may be posing. . . . Am I writing* The Hours *from deep emotion? Of course the mad part tries me so much, makes my mind squint so badly that I can hardly face spending the next weeks at it. . . . I daresay its true, however, that I haven't*

that 'reality' gift. I insubstantise, wilfully to some ex-
tent, distrusting reality—its cheapness. But to get fur-
ther. Have I the power of conveying the true reality?
Or do I write essays about myself? Answer these
questions as I may, in the uncomplimentary sense, &
still there remains this excitement.

—Virginia Woolf's diary entry after Mansfield's
death (this is often quoted as it talked about
The Hours, which was later renamed *Mrs. Dalloway*)

One can go on quoting Woolf's comments from her letters and diaries on Mansfield. There were plenty, some
astute or sympathetic, others unfair, even petty. But of all
Mansfield's notebooks, Woolf only appears twice. In July
1920, there is a simple note, "Virginia, Wed. afternoon."
According to Woolf's diary, the date refers to a lunch at
which the two disagreed on Joseph Conrad's latest book,
The Rescue. "I still maintain that I'm the true seer, the
one independent voice in a chorus of obedient sheep,
since they praise unanimously," Woolf wrote. (One cannot help but wonder whether she would relish her own
future of being in Conrad's position.)

The second time Woolf appears in Mansfield's journal she is not named but only referred to as one of
"that publishing couple in cane chairs." Of course it
can't be said for certain that the couple are the Woolfs.
The description—a character portrait done in dispassion-
ate observation, which was Mansfield's forte—reminds

us of them. A sentence, presumably a compliment to Woolf, stands out: "She was one of those women—one of those women who still exist in spite of everything."

What did Mansfield mean by that? No matter, it does not change the strange satisfaction of a spectator. These two extraordinary women would never know what they had (or had not) said about each other in their private papers. Not knowing transforms them into characters. To see the context of other people's lives when that context is kept away from those who live in it: a reader always wins in the end; a reader has infinite time to interfere with the characters' lives.

Oh, she did put me in her book, but only those quirky moments.

—A writer's mother

Now you've all grown up I don't have anyone to make pancakes for.

—A friend's mother

Everyone can resort to an omniscient voice to tell another person's stories. There is, however, one omniscient voice I cannot live with, yet it is the only voice that continues to drown out others.

Writing is the only part of my life I have taken beyond my mother's storytelling. I have avoided writing in an autobiographical voice because I cannot bear that it could be overwritten by my mother's omniscience. I can easily see all other parts of my life in her narrative: my marriage, my children, my past. Just as she demands to come into my narrative, I demand to be left out of hers. There is no way to change that; not a happy ending, not even an ending is possible.

At a reading given by two writers and attended by their mothers, I watched them occupy the same space with an ease that I envied. There were many things I could have asked them, about reading their children's work and being written into their books. But what I really wanted to know was: What kind of food do you cook for your children?

For as long as I can remember, my mother has never cooked a meal for me. It is a story that cannot be told right in any voice.

> Take a young man, ardent as an Arabian horse, let
> him marry, he is lost. First of all the woman is proud,
> then she is weak, then she faints, then he faints, then
> the whole family faints.
> —Kierkegaard, *Either/Or*

I was reading Kierkegaard while waiting to pick up my children from school. I wished I could wave some mother out of her idling vehicle and show her the passage. Reading, however, is a kind of private freedom: out of time, out of place.

> *When you read a name on an epitaph you are easily*
> *led to wonder how it went with his life in the world;*
> *one would like to climb down into the grave to con-*
> *verse with him.*
>
> —Kierkegaard, *Either/Or*

It is an illusion that writing, like reading, gives one free-dom. Sooner or later people come with their expectations: some demand loyalty; others, to be made immortal as characters. Only the names on the epitaphs remain silent.

> *These stories are dull and tedious as autumn, monoto-*
> *nous in tone, their artistic elements inextricably en-*
> *tangled with the medical, but none of this prevents me*
> *from having the temerity to approach you with a*
> *humble request for your permission to dedicate this*
> *little book to you.*
>
> —Anton Chekhov to Pyotr Tchaikovsky

In October 1889, Chekhov, not yet thirty years old and fairly new to his writing career, wrote to Tchaikovsky about a soon-to-be-published collection. The title was *Gloomy People.*

Under what circumstance can a writer and a reader become contemporaries? Chekhov's invitation was a gesture to abolish the temporal divide. To cross the boundary so that another person's name will remain with one's words—it is almost an inappropriate request, yet the extraordinary justifies the inappropriateness. No friendship can be posthumous.

Reading William Trevor

In retrospect little makes sense—perhaps all stories, rather than *once-upon-a-time,* should start this way.

Shortly after my first book was published, I asked an Irish friend to send a copy with a thank-you note to William Trevor. I considered the note necessary—without his stories mine would not have been written. I wanted to be well mannered, too, so the note was brief and courteous. A few months later, a reply came, graciously written. I framed the letter and hung it in my study. It was uncharacteristic of me—to assign meaning to an object presumes an attachment. It was there as inspiration, I told myself, from someone I aspired to be.

The story might have ended here. I would have continued reading Trevor as I did Turgenev or Hardy: from a distance, which is a prerequisite for unabashed connection. But Turgenev and Hardy could not have written and raised the possibility of meeting in person one day.

The next November, traveling to London for an event, I wrote to Trevor about the possibility of visiting him. It is inconceivable now to think I behaved in such a way, as Trevor is among the most private writers, which was not difficult for me to deduce. I myself would have been taken aback by the inappropriateness of such a request.

THE EFFORT TO avoid isolation sometimes agitates me. The thought of disappearing from the world is an emergency exit, which I agreed to give up when I left the hospital. To think people used to be able to disappear easily: borders crossed, names changed, evidence destroyed, connections severed. No one seems to mind the absence of Miss Havisham or Mrs. Rochester. A father in a Jean Stafford novel walks out of a cobbler's workshop and is never seen again. Maidens from *Dream of the Red Chamber* or *The Tale of Genji,* when heartbroken or abandoned, humiliated or disillusioned, become Buddhist nuns, their stories ending long before their lives do. An uncle, my mother's eldest brother, vanished on the eve of the Communist victory over the Nationalist army, and an orphan girl, half maid and half daughter in the family and raised as his future bride, had to be married off to another man. The aunt in Nanxun, we called her; no other relative was known by the place where he or she lived. In an album there were family pictures she sent each year to my grandfather, all her children having inherited her remarkable beauty, growing up effortlessly in front of my eyes each time I flipped the pages. The aunt in Nanxun was mentioned often because of the unmentionable, an uncle presumably alive in Taiwan on optimistic days, presumably killed in action when optimism could not be sustained. (I learned of his existence and the conjecture of his fate by eavesdropping on my mother and my aunt once. Foolishly I told a friend at school, who then wrote a note to inform the teacher about this uncle of mine in Taiwan. The note was passed on to my mother. The teacher was her colleague, thoughtful enough to intercept a secret that could bring harm, though I could not find gratitude for the teacher nor forgiveness for my friend. It was because of their meddling that I received a beating.)

Forty years later the uncle appeared as unexpectedly as he had disappeared, in a long letter that had taken more than a year, through many hands, to reach his father. My grandfather, with a few months to live, hoped for a reunion with his lost son, but the travel ban across the Taiwan Strait would not be lifted for another two years.

We now live in an ever-connected world, allocated only the wishful thinking of privacy and solitude. Once, when my green card application was denied and it was reported in the news, a man calling himself Doctor S— kept phoning my workplace with a marriage offer, saying it would secure a green card for me. Once a woman said to me at a cocktail party the moment I entered the well-groomed garden: I want you to know, had my mother had your success she would not have killed herself. At a festival in East Sussex I watched a man come up to Trevor afterward and ask if he could stop by for tea, describing Trevor's house correctly and in detail.

IN NOTES SENT to my publisher and to the hotel, Trevor asked me to phone once I arrived in London. A meeting was proposed, not in Devon, where he lives, but in Bath, more easily accessed by train for both parties. It was considerate of him, I knew, but it also occurred to me that Bath would be safer for him to meet a stranger. I could be a character in a Trevor story, quiet and nondescript yet possessing inexplicable malevolence. Can a mistrustful person, who is capable of dissecting herself with ruthless imagination, be trustworthy at all?

It turned out that I could not travel to Bath. There was publicity lined up for the day. I was disappointed but relieved. External interference pardons one from ambivalence. My wish to meet Trevor was as strong as the fear that it might happen—there was no way to rid the doubt that had begun to plague me: Who are you? What makes you think of yourself as innocuous?

I phoned back, with the hope that Trevor would be relieved, too. We chatted about the weather—rain in London and rain in Devon—for a minute. He told me there would be other opportunities. Next year he and his wife were planning to visit America. By ship, he said; I can guarantee you it's a more pleasant way to travel.

. . .

JULY 2015. WE visited China for the first time since my husband and I became American citizens. While in Baishan, my husband's hometown, my mother called and said her brother had died that morning.

Years ago, I had written a novel set in Baishan without having seen it. Baishan, *White Mountain,* used to be Muddy River, named after the river running through town. In the 1990s the city government had deemed the name a hindrance to its prosperity and rechristened the city. With a novelist's opportunism I had claimed the unwanted Muddy River. My husband had drawn a map of the city circa the 1970s, and I had followed people's footsteps in it.

When we entered the city I noticed the bridge where two of my characters met for the first time, the foot of the mountain where a trusting dog was poisoned, the cooling tower of the electricity plant where a murderous janitor worked, and the river itself, befittingly muddy, fast flowing after days of rain. I had wondered if I would notice things about the place and its people that I had not imagined while working on the novel. I did not, which was a disappointment. I do not mind that my imagination is limited; I do mind when the world is not bigger than what one can imagine.

Until the phone call about my uncle's death, I had been dispirited. Please, I ordered my eyes, find one thing that is not anticipated, but everything in China seemed only to confirm. The cabdrivers told political jokes that I had heard twenty years earlier. The pushing crowd made me impatient, and I elbowed queue cutters with an aggressiveness that came back as easily as the rude slang I hurled at them. My children, Western tourists, were continually amused by the inept English translations of public announcements and signs, but to me they were stale jokes. Only once did I stop to appreciate a message. At the Beijing international airport, a woman on a bulletin board encourages her audience to enjoy life. "Take a look at this wonderful life unfolding in front of you," she exhorts in Chinese, but sounds skeptical (or subversive) in the English translation: *This wonderful life lies as you see it.*

THE FIRST STORY I ever read by William Trevor was "Traditions," set in an Irish boarding school. It was published in *The New Yorker* with a photo of young scholars in dark suits as illustration. Its reality was far from mine. I was in a science program then, uncertain if I should continue. My doubt was that I could easily see my life unfurl in front of me: a degree in a year, a few years of post-doctorate training, a secure job in academia or the biomedical industry, a house and children, a dog because a dog rollicking in a neatly maintained yard had always appeared to me to be the pinnacle of an American life.

I checked out *The Hill Bachelors,* Trevor's newest collection, after reading the story, and trudged through the snow from the university library to the student union, where I sat on a green sofa next to a movie theater where films in foreign languages drew a limited crowd every night. Details preserved by memory can be dull, significant only to the one remembering, but it is the mundane that remains mysterious.

It would be presumptuous to claim that a connection was made during that first encounter; it would not be as presumptuous to say a space that had not been known to me was made possible through reading Trevor. From *The Hill Bachelors* I moved on to his other books. A few weeks later I discussed with my advisor the possibility of leaving science. Stay, he said; you have a bright future in this country. Yes, I said, but I can already see myself at the end of that future; I know I will regret it if I don't try this.

This, as I explained to him, was to become a writer. To write is to find a new way to see the world, and I did not doubt, as I was reading Trevor, that I wanted to see as he does.

LETTERS WERE EXCHANGED a few months ahead of Trevor's visit to America to set the date of the meeting. In October 2007, I took a red-eye flight from California to Boston to meet him for lunch. I had three hours, as I was to catch the evening flight back.

Many things were talked about during the lunch: a trip the previous year Trevor and his wife, Jane, had taken to meet the letterer who would carve their gravestones; a conversation decades ago with his father about becoming a letterer himself; a funeral during which religious music had been played against the will of the dead and the alive; a conversation with Graham Greene, another with V. S. Pritchett; descriptions of Molly Keane's work and the graveyard she was buried in, which I would visit the next year. Halfway through the lunch, a woman in an orange blouse walking past the restaurant patio caught Trevor's attention. There was something incomprehensible about her in that moment, he explained. Such moments may pass, he said, though I sensed that often they did not.

After lunch Trevor showed me the work of Henry Moore near his hotel. I followed him, or my eyes followed where I thought he was looking, feeling apprehensive. I could describe the sunny New England afternoon in October and the bronze sculptures surrounded by the trees that were changing colors, but they would be clichés. The truth is, I did not know what I was supposed to see.

THIS APPREHENSION REPEATS itself, in museums and galleries and movie theaters. Once a friend pointed out that a sentence I had written describing a chrysanthemum felt wrong. It's not bad, I said, defending it, not doubting at all that I had made every word right. It was not that the sentence was poorly written, she said, but that it was written not from perception but its absence.

This art of seeing—a painting, a sculpture, a film—is an elusive one to me. In Trevor's novella *Nights at the*

Alexandra, a cinema in a provincial Irish town offers the setting of a tale of love and loyalty. In Trevor's memoir, days are whiled away in cinemas, the boredom of youth compensated by the wonders on screen.

I have never felt the attraction to films. The movie theaters in Beijing—Workers' Clubs they were called in the 1970s and early 1980s, which held over a thousand people—offered little wonder. The newsreels about King Sihanouk and his comrade General Pol Pot were repetitive, and the movies, which we were often required to see as part of school, did not interest me as much as the people sitting nearby, a woman cracking sunflower seeds or a man gurgling while drinking tea from a mug. Often someone would be summoned during a movie. A handwritten note, saying Comrade So-and-So was requested due to an emergency, would be projected onto the dark column next to the screen. These interruptions felt like riddles to which the answers were withheld forever. Obligingly I offered scenarios to satisfy myself. I wished that my name would appear.

One of my most dreaded activities in the army was the weekly movie, an enrichment activity to raise morale. I established a competition with the girl who sat next to me to see who could sleep through these movies longer— I was the more frequent winner. But my feats were not as admirable as those of the girl in another squad, who could stand in the most perfect military posture but doze off confidently.

The girls who slept during the daytime were your allies. After lights-out and before reveille they occupied storage rooms and toilet stalls and memorized English vocabulary. There were other night wanderers, too. Once a girl was found weeping in the darkness; she was later sent home. Once my bunkmate, reputed to be one of the top young mathematicians in China, was stopped by a girl when she went to use the bathroom. The girl had spent hours after lights-out trying to solve a well-known mathematical problem and asked for her help. Crazy, someone commented, but obsessions demanded respect, too. A petite girl in my squad regaled us with stories from her village, where women took their own lives with weed killer and pesticides as readily as—in her exact words— apples dropped from apple trees. The same girl read and marked a few notices in a magazine where young women advertised their wishes to seek soul mates in the army. Lecherous, she called the women; all they want is to marry a solider for practical gain. I was doubtful but persuaded—don't question me, she said; these are people I've grown to know—to draft replies. I made up male names and ranks and combined them with solid knowledge about military life, and mailed the letters in army-issued envelopes to ensure that a reply would come to our fictional selves. For days and weeks we waited. No love letter ever found its way into our hands.

· · ·

ON THE PHONE, reporting my uncle's death, my mother informed me that toward the end of his life he had become violent, beating his children and grandchildren. Your cousins said it was dementia, she said; but do you think what he really had were mental problems?

My mother has a way of talking about mental illness and suicide that makes me uneasy. The day I arrived in Beijing she reported that the father of an elementary-school classmate had died. When his wife was out grocery shopping, he made a detailed list of bank accounts and passwords, bills to be paid and already taken care of, and then hanged himself. Do you remember him? my mother asked. Yes, I said. He was active in the retirees' choir, my mother said; a good tenor. He looked happy, she said; why would he do it? I had no answer, so my mother asked me if she had told me about the death of our former neighbor Mrs. Xiao. Yes, I said, but that did not stop her from telling it again: the woman had jumped from her eighth-floor apartment the year before. Courteous, aloof, elegantly dressed at a time when most women wore gray and blue Mao jackets, she was one of the most graceful people I had known as a child. She had refused to join the neighborhood gossip (and so became a subject); she had never meddled with my or any child's business.

When I was growing up, my family never once traveled together. The summer I was seven, my uncle, who lived four hours by train from Beijing, brought my sister and me to his home, the first time I had been on a train or set foot in another city. Perhaps it is his death that makes me modify the memory, but it seems those two weeks at my uncle's belonged to the happiest time of my childhood. Though I know, in retrospect, that the summer must have been difficult for his family. Our eldest cousin had taken the college entrance exam and scored third in his province, but he had a noticeable limp from polio, so no college would admit him. He was quiet. Still, he showed us around town like a dutiful host, carrying four children on a bike with twenty-eight-inch wheels and reinforced for agricultural use. As he rode across town, my sister and I and our two cousins waved at people as though we were a troupe of acrobats.

My uncle played for hours on a pump organ every evening. I did not understand his music, but I was mesmerized by the pedals going up and down.

When I was in high school, my uncle wrote a long letter to his three nieces narrating his grievances. He was six when the Japanese invaded his hometown, and when his parents evacuated, he was left behind. (Wrong, my mother and my aunt said. The right version, they explained, was that he had been playing with a servant's son, refused to leave, and said he would go to their grandfather's house for a few days; but their grandfather was soon killed by the Japanese, and a few days became a few months.) His parents, he wrote in the letter, never cared for him, and as a teenager he had been forced to seek a future in the army.

(Wrong, my mother and my aunt said. Their big brother, an officer in the Nationalist army, had helped him enroll as a cadet.) Both brothers fought against Mao's army in the civil war. When they lost, one of them crossed the Taiwan Strait, while the uncle who missed the boat was sent to a factory to be reformed. Eventually he became a music teacher in an elementary school. By the time he wrote the letter there were more reasons to wail against life's injustice: his elder brother's prosperity in Taiwan (he himself could've had the same good life had he left China), his son's disability, which made it hard for him to find a wife, his only daughter's stillborn baby. Disappointment after disappointment: Did anyone ever try to understand him? The question upset my aunt and my mother. They decided that he must have gone mad like many before him. Why else would he write such untruths? Doesn't he already have three children to inherit his woes?

In interviews Trevor says that he writes "out of curiosity and bewilderment." What does not make sense is what matters. What motivated my uncle to write the letter? Is it fascination or devotion that makes my mother start her conversations with the news of someone's suicide? Is it selfish of me to react coolly, as though it were irrelevant? Why did Trevor agree to meet me? Why was the lunch with Trevor not a merely courteous meeting where gratitude was properly expressed and accepted? Come and visit before too long, he said, and spoke of the garden he wanted me to see. At the metro station, the man behind me on the escalator turned around to look at Jane, who had joined us, and Trevor. They waved until I was out of sight. A goodbye, isn't it? the man said, and I said a goodbye indeed. More leave-taking would follow in the coming years, at the Exeter train station; at London Victoria; at the sunny garden of a restaurant in Devon. At each farewell the question not asked is always there: Will I see you again?

Only by fully preparing oneself for people's absence can one be at ease with their presence. A recluse, I have begun to understand, is not a person for whom a connection with another person is unattainable or meaningless, but one who feels she must abstain from people because a connection is an affliction, or worse, an addiction. It had not occurred to me, until I met Trevor, to ask: *Will I see you again?* What had precluded me from asking is this: *Perhaps I won't see you again, and if so, goodbye for now and goodbye forever.*

Do you think of your characters after you finish the books? I asked Trevor the next time I visited him, when he was driving me from the train station to his house.

I do, he said. I don't reread them but I remember the characters. I still feel sad for them sometimes. Do you?

I remember your characters and feel sad for them, too, I said.

He looked at me. No, what I mean is, do you think about your characters? Do you feel sad for them?

I knew that was what he had asked, but to admit that characters, having left, still kept me a hostage seemed silly.

It was nearly spring—February, though warm and sunny—and flowers in the garden were already blossoming. At lunch, Trevor placed me on the side of the table facing the window so I could see outside. He sat down, and rose again, pulling the curtain ever so slightly. This way, he explained to me, I could enjoy the garden without the sun shining into my eyes.

Sometimes people ask me what they should read if they want to start reading William Trevor. To say anything about Trevor's work is also to speak about memories—they are in English, and I know where they start. There is "The Piano Tuner's Wives": the pain of seeing the characters struggle with cruelty they do not know they are capable of is not alleviated by familiarity. There is "Reading Turgenev": once in Pennsylvania I was driven by a poet in the moonlit countryside, and she told me that she had been working on a poem called "Reading Turgenev" as a homage. There is *Nights at the Alexandra,* which traveled often with me. Once on a trip to New York, I watched a middle-aged woman and a child on the subway, the girl no more than thirteen, her head on the older woman's shoulder, the latter caressing the child's inner thigh. I could not tell if they were mother and daughter or a pair of lovers. Not knowing disturbed me as much as either possibility. Later in the hotel I started the first paragraphs of a novella. The narrator, a middle-aged woman living by herself in Beijing, tells her story with the same opening lines used by the narrator in Trevor's novella, an older bachelor in a provincial Irish town. A person living in isolation does not speak from solitude, but loneliness; that Trevor's narrator decided to speak to the world makes it possible for the woman to do so.

Trevor's books—*Other People's Worlds, Fools of Fortune, Elizabeth Alone, The Story of Lucy Gault,* and many more—offer me a haven. But even to explain that is to intrude: there is the privacy of Trevor, who has built that space; there is my privacy, too—in writing and in life one is often sustained by memories unshared.

AFTER TREVOR GAVE his last public reading—I had flown to England for it—he told Jane and me about an old man at the end of the book-signing queue. The man had come not for Trevor's signature, but to thank him. His wife had loved Trevor's stories, and when she had become too sick, he read to her. It was a Trevor story he had been reading to her as she died.

In time I would learn what it meant to understand one's own writing through the eyes of a dying reader. A woman from Canada wrote to me, noting the chapter and page number where she had read a sentence that she said she would never want to lose. Her brain had been damaged from radiation, she wrote; she had not been able to concentrate because she fell asleep so often. She felt isolated but did not wish to seek out others. "This is something I have long considered and now I think I have my answer," she said of the sentence. "Perhaps I will never sleep again."

I remembered writing the sentence. Defending my mind at that moment, which was considering death as the way out, I had trespassed the boundary and written about myself: *Love measured by effort was the only love within his capacity. Failure too, measured by effort, would be the failure he would have to make peace with one day.*

THE OTHER DAY I read through the letters from Trevor. I wish there were a way to write them into this book. But I also wish there were a way to leave him unnamed as two other friends are among these pages.

HOW OLD IS your baby? a young woman asked me when, years ago, I checked into my side of the hospital room we were to share. Three days, I said; he was running a fever when we got home so he was readmitted. How old is your baby? I asked. He turned a month yesterday, she said; we're waiting for him to reach five pounds. She was a high school student, and when she was not called away to nurse her baby she studied in bed. After school, a boy her age came to visit, and they huddled in her narrow bed, whispering and giggling. Two days later, the Twin Towers fell, and I spent the day between watching the news and visiting the quarantined baby. In the evening, when I returned to the room, they had changed the channel to the Cartoon Network, watching *Tom and Jerry* with the volume turned low.

The first time I went to Devon a young woman next to me on the train described the boardinghouse she would inherit one day from her grandparents. Her boyfriend was hoping to be hired by the old couple. I imagined them whispering and giggling behind her grandparents' backs, like the new parents from years ago. One's hope for strangers comes more naturally. Perhaps the child in Iowa, a teenager now, still has parents in love with each other. Perhaps the young woman and her boyfriend have settled down in the boardinghouse.

A few years ago, on a flight to London, a woman next to me asked to see the book I was reading and what I was writing in it. I showed her what I had underlined in an Elizabeth Bowen story, when one character asked another: "Has there been anything you have never told me?" *Frightening*, I had written in the margin, and the woman insisted that I write down it's not so *frightening* for Alex, which was her name.

A cabdriver on my latest visit to Devon asked me which was my local prison, Sing Sing or Alcatraz. Alcatraz, I said, and he expressed regret, as I would not have heard of his relative imprisoned in Sing Sing in the

1930s, who had a record of hosting house parties from which people kept disappearing.

It's my Irish guilt that drove me to the West Coast, a cabdriver in California said to me; have you heard of James Michael Curley, my granduncle, the only mayor of Boston who was elected from prison? Take my card, the driver prompted me, and before I exited the car he reminded me to look up his family story, which I dutifully did.

One morning in Washington, D.C., I stood for half an hour with another woman, waiting for the airport counter to open at five o'clock. She was a single mother, and she and her three daughters were on the way to Disneyland. They had packed all their party clothes and gone over a list to unplug everything in the house. They had saved for years to make this trip, the woman said. It's wonderful chatting with you, she said when the counter opened; we should exchange emails.

People like to be asked about their lives. Sometimes they only need someone to listen. There is not a safer way to be out in the world, until listening pulls one into an unsolicited story. "I do not know how much time I have. I am wondering if you are willing to meet and to see if you are interested in my story," a woman with cancer wrote to me. I had thought it was impossible to deny a dying person's wish until the woman wrote again, predicting I would cancel the appointment because she was "inspired by serial killer Dr. Hannibal Lecter character to

become a psychiatrist. Had suicidal and homicidal ide-
ation. Struggled with being kind and evil constantly. Pursued happiness all these years and never found it. Quite
often I wish I had a button to push to kill the entire human
race."

You must protect yourself, a friend warned me. But to
write one has to give up protection fundamentally.

I HAVE NOT forgotten a person who has come into my
life, and perhaps it is for that reason I have no choice but
to live as a recluse. The people I carry with me have lived
out not only their own rations but mine too. To remember is the due a recluse owes the world.

My father and I used to plant string beans in our yard,
their tendrils reaching higher each day on the bamboo
fence. When summer ended an old woman in the neighborhood would snap the beans a few days before we were
ready to harvest. The first time I caught her stealing I was
furious, but my parents said that I shouldn't be because
she had sewn a cotton jacket for me when I was a baby.
Year after year the old woman harvested our beans, and
every time my parents reminded me to be grateful for the
jacket. Then she stopped coming: she had died, and I had
no more reason to feel anything.

Once my grandfather, taking a walk along Garden
Road, felt unwell and was helped by a young soldier. He
became part of the family, an adopted grandson who visited on weekends. After my grandfather's death, he trav-

eled to Beijing with his new bride and stayed with us. My sister and I adored his bride, who was pretty and mild-mannered. The day before their departure, he had to stay overnight in a queue for train tickets, and I caught her crying in the morning when he had not returned. He was only delayed, and they went home happily married. After they left I found a writing pad, the top page ripped away, though I could see the trace of what had been written: an anxious monologue of the bride's, asking herself what his absence meant, why she was left in this vacancy, and how the marriage had come into being in the first place. Years later I underlined in a Bowen novel a passage about a character's "emphatic" pencil, which had left a trace for her daughter to decipher.

WHAT'S THIS ABOUT? my older son asked me when I was watching on the Internet a military parade in Beijing. A celebration of the end of World War II seventy years ago, I said. My great-grandfather died in that war, I said, and immediately regretted sounding like the cabdrivers easily offering inherited family dramas. Which year was that? my son asked. Nineteen thirty-eight, I said. That was the end of the discussion. I did not want to describe the man's death as it had been described to me. He, a fabric merchant in a small town, was forced into hard labor for the Japanese army; he had a limp that made him unable to keep up with the other laborers, and was killed summarily, his torso cut open by a sword. (Having not met the man and not witnessed his death, I had spent much time thinking about him when I was young. His limp reminded me of my limping cousin.)

I don't understand why Trevor still writes about the Troubles, someone in Ireland once said to me. They are old stories, and Ireland has moved on. I can tell you your books have hurt my feelings, a reader, who turned out to have grown up in the same apartment compound I did, announced at a bookstore reading; why do you have to write about China's history; why can't you make me feel proud of being Chinese? But cruelty and kindness are not old stories, and never will be.

In elementary school, a girl's father died suddenly. The next morning, on cleaning duty, I swept my side of the schoolyard and watched her sweep the other side. (It did not occur to me to question why cleaning duty was more important than a father's death or why I did not offer to help her.) She was weeping, her tears falling into a pile of leaves. I wanted to say something to her but did not know what, all the time plagued by a glum concern. She was the other plump girl in my grade; even the meanest boys would leave her alone now, and I would be the only plump girl to be made fun of. I did not recognize the frivolousness of my worry. Though I remember my subsequent thought while watching her: at least she had a reason to cry, and people would understand.

Did I tell you Teacher Sun died? my mother asked me recently. Nobody is going to miss him, she said; bedbound for ten years and nobody felt bad for him then, either. There was no malice in her words. The dead man, my fifth-grade math teacher, had once been known to beat boys in class and put his hands the wrong way on girls' bodies. No parents or teachers or school officials ever intervened. He was a violent man, capable of doing anything to anyone who offended him. One less evil person in the world, my mother said. Her words reminded me of something I had nearly succeeded in forgetting. This teacher used to write problems on the board at the beginning of class and ask me to solve them while he walked between aisles, taking his time to pick out ears to wring. When I finished the problems, having already inflicted pain on a boy or two he would return to the board. Beautiful, he would remark. Despite his cigarette-stained fingers and the sour breath of a smoker behind his sadistic smile, I did not feel repulsed by his approval. Then he would turn and launch a piece of chalk at someone—we all knew it would happen. You, the teacher would say, yes, I'm talking to you, he would stare at the boy marked by the chalk; you'll never understand the beauty of a mind. With those words I was dismissed and sent back to my seat.

Cruelty and kindness, revisited, are not what they appear to be.

When I visited my parents this past summer, in the same apartment I grew up in, I saw a photo of me, taken on my fifth birthday, next to a photo of my mother, taken when she was sixteen. There were other photos of the family, though those two, older than the rest by decades, their subjects captured at a much younger moment, were prominently displayed. I flinched at this shrine of innocence, when neither girl in the pictures had yet caused much damage. My mother had a dreamy laugh, beautiful in a romantic and glamorous way; I was smiling as ordered by the photographer, not precociously but dutifully. What if I had not known either of them? I would have looked at them more closely, my curiosity not different from my curiosity about any stranger. No better and no worse than others, these two are fools of fortune, too.

"You may be less confused than you imagined," in a letter Trevor wrote. "Stories are a hope, and often they obligingly answer questions."

WHO ARE YOU? Trevor asked when I saw him this past spring. It's okay, I said; I'm only coming to see you. Ah, we met in Boston, he said a minute later. Yes, we met in Boston, I said, but I could have also said: we are solitary travelers, having crossed paths in the land of stories.

Afterword

On Being a Flat Character,
and Inventing Alternatives

There are many ways to answer the question. Not everyone would ask, but some would if true curiosity—a genuine desire to understand—were allowed in place of good manners. I would, too. In fact, I still do ask myself: What made you think suicide was an appropriate, even the only, option?

Various hypotheses have been offered by this or that person at this or that moment: genes, lack of mental strength or maturity, selfishness, cell signals gone randomly awry. There are more practical explanations too. I was once ambitious—or greedy—enough to want to excel at being a mother and a writer while holding a full-time job. For almost ten years I wrote between midnight and four o'clock in the morning.

Would I have deprived myself of such a basic necessity had I known it would leave such damage? I think so. I do not see another way to manage what I wanted to do. In her notes on writing novels, Elizabeth Bowen emphasized alternatives:

> It's the palpable presence of the alternatives that gives action interest. Therefore, in each of the characters, while he or she is acting, the play and pull of alternatives must be felt. . . . By the end of a novel the character's alternatives, many at the beginning, have been reduced to none. . . . The "flat" character has no alternatives.

I WOULD LIKE to believe that there are as many alternatives in life as in fiction; that roads not taken, having once been weighed as options, define one as much as the irreversible direction of the chosen path. What would have become of you had you not left China? asks a friend; what would have become of you had you not landed in Iowa City, or had you stayed a scientist? What I can offer are not alternatives, only negatives. I would not have chosen English as my natural language; I would not have known one can go to school for writing; I would not have become a writer.

But what would have become of me? When this friend asks a similar question about a character—how would her life have turned out had she not emigrated?—I have no trouble seeing her in Beijing: the overpass she crosses every day to get to her bus stop; the crippled beggars she, having at last mastered the art of not looking, no longer gives money; the cabdriver she halfheartedly engages in conversation when he, like all cabdrivers in Beijing, takes pleasure in mocking the government; the many keys on her key ring—one unlocking the wooden box next to her apartment door, in which is the daily delivery of fresh milk for her child (her child would not grow up knowing the joy of walking to the milk station every evening); another one for the mailbox (years ago all mail for the building was crammed into the same green box, an enticement because she always liked to see who were the lucky ones to receive letters); keys for the apartment and the office and the car and the security gates—keys, too many, representing privileges and responsibilities. In my Chinese life I had only one memorable key—the kind that could be found in any antique store in America—bronze, the length of my entire palm, which I carried around my neck on blue nylon twine.

That this character has left Beijing does not change the fact that there is a space for her there. She may refuse to occupy it but it cannot be filled by others. The rowboat on the lake of the Summer Palace, which she could have rented for an afternoon, will stay idle, the oars unhooked from their hinges. Her local postman, the green canvas bag attached to the crossbar of his bicycle, will balance himself with a leg on the curb while sorting the mail, though she will not be there to chat with him. At a class reunion an old, one-inch school picture will be scanned and enlarged because she does not wish to attend or send a current photo to absolve her absence.

Why will you not acknowledge you could be that person—I can hear my friend question me—in fact, you are that person? The answer, I think, is that I do not want a self watching itself and contemplating alternatives. One risks losing one's privacy in fiction, and to be anti-autobiographical lessens that danger. I cannot possibly be any one of my characters; they have alternatives that I do not. And yet I don't mind experiencing their loss of alternatives alongside them. One lives more feelingly in a borrowed life.

Do you not worry about losing your privacy in these essays? again I hear my friend question, but the truth is, the privacy I cling to has little to do with others. Once I saw a preschooler, my son's playmate, demonstrate that skill. He was bothered by a small disaster and, without complaining or crying, he made his body still; his eyes, grayish blue, became lifeless. I had never witnessed so closely a mind switched off by will. It took a few seconds— not long, though a gap nevertheless—for his eyes to turn from panic into glassiness, behind which I could sense that unwavering determination for absence. Practitioners of that vanishing act develop the belief—illusion, really— that one can exist unobserved.

. . .

ONE CANNOT BE an adept writer of one's life; nor can one be a discerning reader of that tale. Not equipped with a novelist's tools to create plots and maneuver pacing, to speak omnisciently or abandon an inconvenient point of view, to adjust time's linearity and splice the less connected moments, the most interesting people among us, I often suspect, are flatter than the flattest character in a novel. Not only do we not have any alternatives, we discredit them. *It has to be so*—this indisputable conviction is often at the foundation of our decisions, including the most impulsive or the most catastrophic. It is easier to be certain of one thing than to be uncertain of a hundred; easier for there to be one *is* than many *might have beens.*

You should be very careful every day for the rest of your life, a doctor told me. Why? I asked. (I could not help but think how bad that line was—*every day for the rest of your life.* Such absoluteness. In fiction a character should never be allowed to speak the line.) Things could sneak up on you, the doctor said; when you realize it you'd have already lost the solid ground underneath you. What do I do? I asked. The doctor answered that I should never go off medication. I understood it as there is nothing I can do.

Does it have to be so? I often wonder.

These essays were started with mixed feelings and contradictory motives. I wanted to argue against suicide as much as for it, which is to say I wanted to keep the option of suicide and I wanted it to be forever taken away from me. Writing this book has taken about two years now, as long as the period that led to it, a year of descending into the darkest despair and a year of being confined by that despair. The bleakness, which can be summarized with a few generic words—suicide attempts and hospitalizations—was so absolute that it sheds little light on things. A sensible goal is to avoid it.

I have learned, during these past few years, that a small misstep can lead to an unraveling, in a matter of hours, sometimes minutes. Wisdom or mental strength is not what is lacking when this happens. To acknowledge that it is not a failure does not mitigate the grief. The difficult moment is not when one gives up—giving up, in fact, brings certainty; relief and peace, too—but afterward, when the same pattern repeats itself. Why, one asks again and again and again, but to question is to confront the unchangeable. One can only accept that cell signaling works faster and in a less regulated manner than logic. Those few seconds before the boy's eyes turned dim: that gap between clarity and confusion is where a mind, with the instinct of self-preservation, battles against itself. That gap is my privacy. Writing fiction has been my way to protect it, though not always effectively. Writing from the gap—this book—is an experiment in establishing a truce with what cannot be changed.

Many drafts were written when things began to feel unbearable. Composing a sentence is better than composing none; an hour taken away from treacherous rumination is an hour gained; following the thread of a thought to the end is better than having many thoughts entangled. In a sense, writing becomes the effort of detecting a warning sign before it appears. There are moments when it must sound as though I am arguing against hope and happiness, against others and myself, but any attachment, even to the most fallacious idea, is an anchor when solidness cannot be felt.

THE PARAGRAPHS IN Montaigne's essays all bear a letter (A, B, or C) to indicate the different time points when he composed them—he often returned to work on the same essays. Without these markers, a reader "may write him off as irresponsibly inconsistent," explains his translator Donald Frame, as the essays "are intended to be a record of change."

It would be presumptuous to mark my essays similarly, though the two years spent writing them have been full of ambiguities. Sentences and paragraphs were written and rewritten under different circumstances, arguments reframed, thoughts revised; most of these essays took a year or longer to write. Coherence and consistency are not what I have been striving for.

There is no ladder out of any world; each world is rimless—my friend Amy Leach writes. A ladder is no longer what I am seeking. Rather, I want one day to be able to say to myself: Dear friend, we have waited this out.

A Partial List of Books

Persuasion, Jane Austen

Sense and Sensibility, Jane Austen

The Death of the Heart, Elizabeth Bowen

To the North, Elizabeth Bowen

People, Places, Things: Essays by Elizabeth Bowen, ed. Allan Hepburn

Elizabeth Bowen, Victoria Glendinning

Selected Stories of Anton Chekhov, trans. Richard Pevear and Larissa Volokhonsky

A Life in Letters, Anton Chekhov, ed. Rosamund Bartlett, trans. Rosamund Bartlett and Anthony Phillips

Autobiography of Maxim Gorky: My Childhood, In the World, My Universities, trans. Isidor Schneider

Monsignor Quixote, Graham Greene

Ways of Escape: An Autobiography, Graham Greene

Jude the Obscure, Thomas Hardy

Life's Little Ironies, Thomas Hardy

The Mayor of Casterbridge, Thomas Hardy

Tess of the D'Urbervilles, Thomas Hardy

Letters of Emma and Florence Hardy, ed. Michael Millgate

Ernest Hemingway: Selected Letters 1917–1961, ed. Carlos Baker

Either/Or: A Fragment of Life, Søren Kierkegaard

Letters to Monica, Philip Larkin, ed. Anthony Thwaite

Stories, Katherine Mansfield

The Katherine Mansfield Notebooks, ed. Margaret Scott

Katherine Mansfield: Selected Letters, ed. Vincent O'Sullivan

All Will Be Well: A Memoir, John McGahern

Amongst Women, John McGahern

By the Lake, John McGahern

The Collected Stories, John McGahern

Elbow Room, James Alan McPherson

Hue and Cry: Stories, James Alan McPherson

A Region Not Home: Reflections from Exile, James Alan McPherson

The Complete Essays of Montaigne, trans. Donald M. Frame

Marianne Moore: Complete Poems

Marianne Moore: Selected Letters, ed. Bonnie Costello

Holding On Upside Down: The Life and Work of Marianne Moore, Linda Leavell

Strong Opinions, Vladimir Nabokov

Jean-Christophe, Romain Rolland, trans. Gilbert Cannan

Letters from a Stoic, Seneca, trans. Robin Campbell

War and Peace, Leo Tolstoy, trans. Richard Pevear and Larissa Volokhonsky

Dream Tales and Prose Poems, Ivan Turgenev, trans. Constance
   Garnett
Fathers and Sons, Ivan Turgenev, trans. Richard Freeborn
First Love and Other Stories, Ivan Turgenev, trans. Richard Free-
   born
Home of the Gentry, Ivan Turgenev, trans. Richard Freeborn
Rudin, Ivan Turgenev, trans. Richard Freeborn
Sketches from a Hunter's Album, Ivan Turgenev, trans. Richard
   Freeborn
Spring Torrents, Ivan Turgenev, trans. Leonard Schapiro
The Gentle Barbarian: The Work and Life of Turgenev, V. S. Pritch-
   ett
Turgenev: His Life and Times, Leonard Schapiro
Turgenev's Letters: A Selection, ed. and trans. Edgar H. Lehrman
Letter from an Unknown Woman, Stefan Zweig, trans. Anthea Bell
*Stefan and Lotte Zweig's South American Letters: New York, Ar-
   gentina and Brazil, 1940–42,* ed. Darién J. Davis and Oliver
   Marshall

AND I'M INDEBTED to William Trevor and all his books.

Acknowledgments

My deepest gratitude to Sarah Chalfant and Jin Auh for being everything for me and my books: friends, readers, and advocates. I would like to thank the Wylie Agency, especially Charles Buchan and Jacqueline Ko, for their tireless work on my behalf.

As always, I would like to thank Kate Medina for her faith in my books. I would like to thank Simon Prosser for his insight and precision.

Friends whose support has been essential—Mona Simpson, Elizabeth McCracken, Duchess Goldblatt, Patrick Cox, Lan Samantha Chang, Connie Brothers, Stuart Dybek, Chen Reis, Rabih Alameddine, and Tom Drury— thank you for being my friends.

Love to my parents and my sister.

To Patricia and Patrick Hughes: you have shown me things I did not understand and things I thought impossible.

Dearest Amy Leach: Where do I even start? Neither you nor I will, for all the tea in China, become a whateverist—what joy, what solace, what good fortune it is to be sensible and nonsensical together.

What anchors you? This question has been asked again and again, and the answer has never changed: my husband and my children. You help me take myself seriously.

ABOUT THE AUTHOR

YIYUN LI is the author of four works of fiction: *Kinder Than Solitude, The Vagrants, A Thousand Years of Good Prayers,* and *Gold Boy, Emerald Girl.* A native of Beijing and a graduate of the Iowa Writers' Workshop, she is the recipient of many awards, including a PEN/Hemingway Award, a Benjamin H. Danks Award from the American Academy of Arts and Letters, and a MacArthur Foundation fellowship. Her work has appeared in *The New Yorker, A Public Space, The Best American Short Stories, The Best American Essays,* and *The O. Henry Prize Stories,* among other publications. She was named by *The New Yorker* as one of the "20 Under 40" fiction writers to watch. Her books have been translated into more than twenty languages. She teaches creative writing at the University of California, Davis, and lives in Oakland, California, with her husband and their two sons.

yiyunli.com

ABOUT THE TYPE

This book was set in Sabon, a typeface designed by the well-known German typographer Jan Tschichold (1902–74). Sabon's design is based upon the original letter forms of sixteenth-century French type designer Claude Garamond and was created specifically to be used for three sources: foundry type for hand composition, Linotype, and Monotype. Tschichold named his typeface for the famous Frankfurt typefounder Jacques Sabon (c. 1520–80).